The
Psychology
of Color
and Design

The Psychology

nh Nelson-Hall, Chicago
Professional/Technical Series

of **Color** and Design

Deborah T. Sharpe

Library of Congress Cataloging in Publication Data

Sharpe, Deborah T
    The psychology of color and design.

    (Professional/technical series)
    Includes bibliographical references.
    1. Color—Psychology. I. Title.
    BF789.C7S48   152.1'45   73-91308
    ISBN 0-88229-107-6

Manufactured in the United States of America

To Clifford—
Who would have been
the proudest of all

Table of contents

Preface   ix
1/Historic aspects of color   1
2/Color and children   7
3/Culture and color   33
4/Color and personality   53
5/The perception of color   81
6/Gestalt and color   101
7/Applied color   113
Notes   143
Name index   159
Subject index   163

Preface

As one of the few scientifically trained psychologists working in the commercial field of color, I have received thousands of letters requesting information on the psychology of color. Since I have been unable to correspond with all of these people—teachers, students, psychologists, psychiatrists, sociologists, designers, artists, architects, and others—I am writing this book.

Available information in this area tends to be either highly esoteric and technical or scientifically unreliable because it's relative to a particular time. Many studies utilize the results of opinion polls or market research. Such data reflect color fads and frills and are frequently obsolete by the time the book is in print. To report market research in scientific clothing is a deception and a disservice. Other books on color present little or no documentation or reference to classic studies.

In contrast, this book explores the central issues and the large body of solid knowledge that now exists on the science of color. The major areas that I write about are the historical and cultural aspects of color, the interaction of personality and color, psychological insights into the perception and use of color, and the practical applications of the science of color. The results of major tests, like the Rorschach, that utilize human responses to color are also reported. By showing that a sizable body of research does exist, I hope others will be motivated to add to this store of information.

People attach all kinds of different meanings to colors. In general, laymen tend to think that there are strong relationships between the colors a person prefers for his clothing, home furnishings, the objects that surround him, and the traits of his personality. Indeed, this is true, but one must exercise extreme caution against making quick generalities based on superficial evidence. On the other hand, there are designers and other professionals who feel that the use of certain colors at certain times will produce certain kinds of behavior. There are almost as many theories in this area of study as there are practitioners. Again, one must be wary of facile judgment.

It will be my task in this volume to separate fact from fancy, the old wives' tales from the plain truth. One hypothesis that will be supported, for instance, is that color responses are more tied to man's emotions than to his intellect. In general, people do not respond to colors with their minds.

To begin, if response to color is to have any meaning for the reader, some understanding of an underlying theory is essential. A survey of the books and articles in the field, my own studies of color responses and color preferences in relation to measures of personality, interests, and intelligence quotients, and the studies by E. Schachtel and Maria Rickers-Ovsiankina, all lead to a theory that, though not entirely psychoanalytic, does lend itself most appropriately to psychoanalytic explanation.

The theory is that color and affect experiences are essentially passive and detached. "Passive" refers to the relation between color affect and ego, and not to overt behavior in the presence of color. While perhaps not the ideal word to use here, "passive" does convey the meaning most appropriately, even though most people perceive of color responses as active and participatory. Thus, color responses are normally under the control of the ego, which is defined as the self-preserving, socialized, conscience-controlled energy system, as opposed to the id, which is the primitive, instinctual energy system from which the ego was originally differentiated.

An individual's response to color gives insight into the development of his ego, and conversely, the strength of id control. In fact, one could almost postulate a tug of war between the ego and the id as color responses become strong, which is in keeping with the Freudian concept of tensions between the energy systems as each tries to gain control. In man's inner life the primitive drives are lined up against the socialized, disciplined drives.

E. Schachtel describes the experience of color and that of affect as that of "the immediacy of the relation of the object-subject."[1] He implies that the unstimulated organism is in a "resting state," or perhaps a state of equilibrium, and that the response to stimuli will be mediated by the degree of either ego control or id control. Dr. Rickers-Ovsiankina describes color response as a measure of the degree of permeability of the boundary between the ego and the outside world.[2] More recent studies suggest a somewhat broader approach, in which the response to, or the emotional handling of, color reflects the degree of the individual's emotional control and social orientation. The person who readily responds to his external environment is color-oriented; the person who readily responds to his internal drives and feelings is less color-oriented.

K. Warner Schaie has described the different modes of response to color as differentiated, restricted, and diffuse.[3] The individual with a normal balance between ego and id control exhibits a differentiated response; that is, he likes several colors and is generally consistent about these preferences. The individual with a restricted color response, who likes one or two colors to the exclusion of all others, has an overdeveloped superego, and in general would be rigid, moralistic, and lacking in flexibility. The individual with diffuse color responses, who "loves" all or many colors with the same degree of enthusiasm, is under the dominance of his id energy system, and in general would be impulsive, fractionated, and given to following his instincts. The diffuse individual often tends to be controlled by his environment, shifting and changing as it dictates, permitting others to determine his behavior. His own emotional drives will be released in a relatively random manner, and he will often be unable to interpret the emotions of others.

Along with several other investigators into the color phenomenon, I have found an increase of color usage and response in recent years in the "normal," well-adjusted individual. This general change in color response can be attributed to a decrease of structure in our society and, particularly, to the color explosion of the 1960s.

The above theory explains color preferences and responses primarily in relation to personality structure; however processes of growth, development, genetics, environment, and experience are incorporated into the underlying processes that account for the differentiated personality orientation, thus making it possible to study the effects of these various factors and their influences in a variety of ways and stages.

The interested reader will find few, if any, books on the library shelves that consider the broad psychological aspects of color in scientific depth. There are many books on the technical aspects of light, hue, saturation, and the like, but not many responsible writers have dared to get too far away from the definite conclusions of the physics laboratory. This book is an attempt to break new ground, hopefully in an effective, logical manner. There may be times when the reader may feel that I am not plowing a straight furrow, that I have strayed from my original point of reference. My only response here would be a plea to exercise patience, to see the book through to its final conclusions. This subject is so wide-ranging, so fraught with new insights, that it would be a disservice to all concerned to treat it in a constricted manner.

1/Historic aspects of color

The history of response to color goes back as far as man himself. Primitive man reacted to the many colors he saw in nature—from budding flowers to waning sunsets. First he used biological color as a means of survival, for identifying objects and animals as friends or foes. He even began quite early in history to adapt color to his own uses—in his cave paintings, in some of his attire, and most especially as symbols of his inner life. An entire book could be written about the various attitudes toward color and its uses in early religions. Aristotle was the first philosopher to posit a systematic theory of color; though unlike his other writings, it holds little relevance for modern man.

Color, of course, is not a separate and distinct field of study; it is a vast, complex area, touching almost all fields from sociology to music, from painting to physics. Most of the early work in the field was done by philosophers and artists. From before the time of Leonardo da Vinci, artists have held their own theories of color. Many of these theories have interest and merit

1

for the modern student, but their common fault is that they are based on one man's trial and error rather than on rigorous scientific investigation. Many of them are quite personal, having been formulated in response to the needs of one man's art. Sir Isaac Newton brought the resources of the developing science of physics to bear on the problem of color and developed his law of color mixture. Early in the nineteenth century, the German poet Goethe gave his views on color harmony and on the symbolic values of the various colors in his book, *Farbenlehre*.[1] While his scientific information can certainly be called into question in light of modern discoveries, his work on the subjective experience of color remains quite valid.

One obvious fault with Goethe's work is that he dealt only with hues—what color was being perceived; he failed to consider brightness. (Was the color dull or was it sharp and clear?) And saturation. (Was the color shallow and wishy-washy, or was it deep and strong?) These three elements, hue, brightness, and saturation, are used throughout this book since every modern color theoretician has recognized their importance. Goethe did suggest that red, yellow, and orange—the colors at the warm end of the spectrum—are exciting, vital, forthcoming (or advancing) colors, while blue, green, and purple—the colors at the cool end of the spectrum—induce a muted response, a comfortable, perhaps even soothing approach to the situation at hand. In broad terms, this is certainly in accord with what we have found to be true about color today.

Throughout history, there have been various obstacles that have made it difficult for anyone—artist, physicist, philosopher, or whomever—to formulate an adequate theory of color. For instance, before the middle of the nineteenth century, there were not many good, reliable, consistent dyes, and the best available dyes were rather costly. In the early days, color was produced by natural pigments, which were not soluble. Today the colorist has at this fingertips a tremendous variety of soluble chemical dyes.

At the end of the nineteenth century, some important work began in both affective reactions to color and the realm of color aesthetics. The Frenchman Chevreul introduced the idea of classification into harmonies of analogy and harmonies of contrast. These harmonies were classified in terms of hue, brightness, and saturation.[2] Bezold (1874) and Brucke (1887) set forth the position that neighboring hues and hues that are complementary, or almost so, can be used together in harmony. On a color wheel of 12 hues, a difference of less than one step provides harmony, and a difference of more than one-third of the circle also yields pleasing color harmony. In-between areas were not felt to offer pleasing harmonies at all.

There were some early laboratory experiments that tested color preferences. In 1894, J. Cohn, a member of Wundt's laboratory, worked with a limited number of colors shown on papers a few inches square. In general, strongly contrasting pairs were preferred by his subjects. The succeeding quarter century or so was marked by many similar investigations designed to ascertain the color preferences of all kinds of people. But this work was hampered by several factors: color samples, for instance, were not standardized, so that different swatches of the same color from the same manufacturer were not exactly the same. Viewing conditions, especially light, were extremely varied, and sometimes they were inadequate.

Nor was everyone happy with the results that were obtained. In 1925, Gustav von Allesch stated that all hope of finding consistent reactions to colors would have to be abandoned.[3]

In the field of color harmony, progress was being made at a good rate, although no scientific theory in this area was really possible until there was a standard method of color specification. In 1931, the Commission Internationale de l'Eclairage (CIE) promulgated a method of color designation that, at the time, represented a great leap forward. It was not an ideal system for color harmony work because equal distances in CIE space do not correspond to equal perceptual steps in color. However, it did more or less prepare the way for later work by Munsell[4] and Ostwald,[5] each of whom developed color solids independent of each other, the former in the United States and the latter in Germany. Ostwald's theory that any orderly arrangement of colors is harmonious was quite advanced for its time and is quite close to contemporary ideas on the subject—much closer than Munsell's.

Modern theories of color harmony are based essentially on a geometric form on which a great many colors can find a place. Thus color harmony can be reduced to a mathematical equation, similar to the problems that can be worked out in solid geometry. As will be explained later in the book, while these various systems of color harmony are extremely helpful—if only in defining various colors—they do not offer the full answer to the question of what color is best in a particular situation. The solid geometry of color harmony quantification was cracked apart by the color revolutions of the post-World War II era, and it will never be the same again.

A great deal of research has been devoted to ascertaining color affections, color preferences, and color meanings. Some observers, such as J. P. Guilford,[6] suggest a physiological basis, but most psychologists feel that the subject is too complicated to yield to such a simple explanation. An interesting series of experiments was undertaken by Edward Bullough in 1908.[7] As his subjects gave judgments on colors, they seemed to divide into the following four categories: the objectives, who evaluated the colors based on finite attributes such as saturation and brightness; the associatives, who linked the colors with various external objects; the physiologicals, who were affected emotionally by the colors; and the characters, who responded to color based on what might be called its mood. Since Bullough's time, more observers have agreed that different people look at colors in different ways.

In 1934, Albert R. Chandler made an important contribution by formulating a developmental hierarchy for experimentation on color, encompassing primary factor, primary effects, and secondary effects.[8] Color effects, he said, "are never absolute but are relative to the total situation." At about the same time, it was becoming clear that only those colors that attract a person's attention are important to him. Also, the concept of synesthesia, where sensations in one field are linked to those in another field, began to get some attention. Colors, for instance, proved to have temperature ("cool") and weight ("heavy"), and were even related to sound ("loud") and smell ("fresh").

In 1959, Harry Helson promulgated his adaptation level theory of human behavior, a level such that "stimuli above adaptation reflectance are tinged with the hue of the illuminant, stimuli below adaptation levels are tinged with the after-image complementary to the hue of the illuminant, and stimuli at or near adaptation reflectance are either achromatic or weakly saturated color of uncertain hue." This complex theory recognizes the fact that the experimental approach to aesthetics involves a large number of variable factors.[9]

There is some doubt that science will ever be able to quantify or predict aesthetic values. The goal may never be reached, but advancing the state of knowledge just a little bit is its own reward.

2/Color and children

Because of their limited life experience, children are frequently used in testing to determine the influences of genetics, learning, association, conditioning, development, and experience. In addition, longitudinal studies, which repeat the same experiment on the same children after a uniform interval of time, permit assessment of the developmental features of perceptual and cognitive functioning. Using the data from these studies, educators and parents can plan more effective learning programs and life experiences for each step in the maturing child's life.

Color is an important element in evaluating child development. Various color-form preference categorization tests are among the most frequently used measures of the abstraction phenomenon, the ability to single out specific elements from a pattern on the basis of similar factors. This ability gives an indicator of growing maturity and provides inferences regarding personality organization and intellectual functioning and can be used as a means to assess development across differing backgrounds.

THE PSYCHOLOGY OF COLOR AND DESIGN

The classic color-form preference measure is one in which the subject chooses between two alternatives to match a series of objects against a standard. Objects of the same form are different in color, and those of the same color are different in form. The subject must choose between matching either on the basis of color or on the basis of form. These exercises are done in many variations, such as puzzles, representational figures, and the introduction of the concepts of size and number—the diversity is limited only by the experimenter's imagination and ingenuity. Most of these studies have focused on children between the ages of three to six or seven, the age span during which the critical shift is made from color dominance to form dominance, with preference for form steadily increasing into adulthood.

The shift from color dominance to form dominance does not happen in a rigid lockstep manner, but one dimension is usually preferred twice as often as the other at any given point in a child's development. Similarly, the fact that one child shows an increasing preference for form during a certain age span does not mean that all children will develop a greater preference for form during that same age period. Most children are unidimensional, and children showing mixed dominance are thought to be in a period of transition. Most children reach the peak of color dominance around four and one-half, but about 10 percent of this age group shows pure form dominance. These form-dominant children are said to be intellectually brighter than those showing color or mixed dominance. The median age of transition from color to form dominance is about five, and form dominance usually is established by the age of nine. Since maturation is never a smooth process, there are various color-form levels of abstractions within any group.

It should be noted that some investigations have found children below the age of three to be form dominant, with some as young as six months giving evidence of fine-form discrimination. As for color, some infants as young as four months have shown a preference for red and blue over yellow and gray. Others have shown awareness of the difference between intensities of the same hue. Because of the difficulty of testing infants and children below the age of two, conclusions for these groups are usually presented in cautious terms. Nevertheless, it can be stated that the peaks in the form-color curve occur at twenty-two months for form dominance, at four and one-half years for color dominance, and a reversal to form dominance again from the age of six into adulthood.

The introduction of size, number, and representational figures (animal, house, tree, and the like) into the form-color tests represents a higher level of symbolization and verbalization. At the preschool level, for instance, the choice between form and size favors form at all levels. In the choice between color and size, color was most frequently chosen at the lower age level, with size becoming the dominant response with increased age.

Several investigations have been made of number as a third factor in color-form categorization with children between the ages of seven and ten. The results generally show that as age increases, form dominance increases over color, and number dominance increases over both form and color dominance.

In an effort to parcel out color or form dominance, various representational colored pictures have been shown to preschool children with the request that they match a model. The results indicate that although the "relative objective obtrusiveness" of color or form is generally the determining factor in what will be abstracted, color tends to be the dominant factor with preschool children.[1] On the other hand, when children over the age of seven are presented with representations of familiar objects, neither color nor form nor size is normally the basis of conceptual similarity. By this time, the representational dimension has become the dominant basis of categorization. These results are in keeping with the developmental pattern of the increasing importance of "meaningfulness" at this age level.

Most of the earlier studies on color-form influence were limited mainly to the perception of color and form and did not examine how the child might use these two elements in tests of deeper involvement. Subsequently, puzzles have been designed to help in this area. One of the earliest examples of this technique used a one-color puzzle to measure form dimensionality and one of several colors to assess both color and form dimensionality. The results followed the same pattern as the less complicated measures; that is, nursery school children compared favorably with third graders in handling the one-color puzzles, but there was a dramatic change in favor of the older group in working the color interaction puzzle.

K. W. Schaie administered the Color Pyramid Test (see page 64) to over 800 children from kindergarten through the twelfth grade and scored them according to color and form dominance.[2] The results indicated that a "significant developmental increment of form dominance was found up to age thirteen for boys and to age fourteen for girls." In a comparison group of college sophomores, he found that the "form level of college students was equal to or above that found in adolescence."

Perceptual and cognitive developmental features have also been assessed by many researchers using the Rorschach Inkblot Method (see page 27): the results have consistently shown that pure color responses (C) dominate among young children, color-form responses (CF) dominate in the older child (C responses drop off rapidly), and at a later stage of childhood through adolescence and into adulthood, form-color responses (FC) are dominant. It appears that color develops from an immediate experience that dominates the perception to one where it is integrated with form.

A review of the various techniques used to measure color-form dominance indicates that it does not matter whether the assessing instrument is simple or complex—the results are always the same. However, the fun-and-games features of the puzzles, sorting, and representational materials offer obvious advantages.

Explanations for the shifting color-form dominance phenomenon include maturation, increased personality differentiation from the affective to the intellectual, increased meaningfulness of the environment in terms of utility, less concern for primitive characteristics, increased verbal skills, and introduction to reading and writing. Form dominance, according to some investigators, is a genetically higher level of response than color.

Since approximately 90 percent of the adult population is form dominant, color-dominant persons have been referred to as deviates. One of the most widely held theories underlying these preference patterns states that since color is a primitive response, the adult color-dominant personality tends to be impulsive, immature, egocentric, and less intelligent than the form-dominant personality, which is said to be stable, socially controlled, and mature.

Other theories attribute greater creativity and flexibility to the color-dominant than to the form-dominant personality. Beyond that, since most measures of intellectual ability rely heavily on form and its many facets, it is questionable how valid these tests can be in measuring the intellectual ability of the color-dominant person. And if creativity is a major feature of the color-dominant, and intelligence tests often show a negative correlation with creative ability, then these tests would be inappropriate instruments to use in work with color-dominant persons. The truth probably lies somewhere in the middle of the general mix of all these theories.

Personality correlates of CF persons have been assessed for several college populations. The results of these studies show that color-dominant persons tend to be highly sensitive, individualistic, shy, and somewhat impractical, whereas the form-dominant tend to be more practical, thorough, and conforming. Deaf preschool and deaf young children in general show a preference for color over form. In fact, when deaf and normal children are asked to discriminate among stimuli on the basis of color, the deaf do so significantly better than normal children.

Thus color proves to be a significant element in personality. Just as color is useful for researchers as a tool in personality inventories, so it can help the layman understand how color influences various facets of the child's experience, such as his education and home life.

A knowledge of how children respond to the dimensions of color content, style, and harmony in paintings gives a developmental pattern that makes it possible for both parents and educators to plan meaningful aesthetic experiences. Orange tends to be the favorite color in paintings for those aged three to about six; pink and red follow orange as favorite colors. Animals are favorite subjects, and color is strongly preferred over black. Children appear to be sensitive to color harmony as early as age four, though it is not until the ages between eight and twelve that color harmony becomes a feature of artistic analysis, and even by age twelve this type of appreciation has not yet reached the adult level.

One of the most ambitious studies of aesthetic preferences in children was conducted in France by Pavel Machotka, who studied boys aged six to twelve.[3] He compared the aesthetic developmental steps of content, color, and form with Piaget's three major steps in intellectual development, which are: "(1) that of preoperational thought, between four and seven years, in which notions of classes of objects, of relations between classes, of the conservation of quantity and other extensities, are highly rudimentary; (2) that of concrete operations (ages seven or eight to eleven or twelve), during which classes [of objects] become stable, various extensities become conserved, and the intellectual operations by which conservation is made possible become reversible; and (3) that of formal operations (after eleven or twelve), in which the operations characterizing the previous stage become fully mental, independent of concrete illustration."[4]

The results of Machotka's study indicate that subject matter and color are the criteria by which the beginning school-child up to age seven or eight evaluates paintings. There are two kinds of subject matter: the first, self-identification or subjectivity, is found in children of all ages; the second, where there is an objective, global content, begins to be perceived about age twelve. True to the declining color preference with increasing age, the evaluation of a painting on the basis of a single color declines. The level of evaluation is compared to Piaget's first step in intellectual development. The second step is the one in which evaluation is based on realistic representation, clarity of presentation, and contrast and harmony. Clarity appears to be a frequent mode of evaluation around the age of nine, preceding both contrast and harmony. The third step follows, and is characterized by, an evaluation based on style, composition, and luminosity.

Most of the studies on children's preferences among paintings consistently show that younger children prefer paintings based on subject matter and color without regard to the degree of realism apparent; older children select paintings based on realistic representation, often with some attention focused on harmony and contrast. Adults, especially college graduates and those exposed to art, tend to select on the basis of artistic style.

Young children express their emotions in their paintings. Their first representation is of themselves with an exaggeration by size or number—head, eyes, body, and so on—of those parts that are especially important to them. As the child grows into adolescence, his artistic expression becomes more objective and realistic, although feelings about these objects vary with the individual.

Noting that preschool children express themselves generally at the abstract, nonrepresentational level and reveal more of their affective lives than older children, Alschuler and Hattwick did an extensive study of expressive outlets of two-, three-, and four-year-old children in easel painting, crayons, clay, blocks, and dramatic play.[5] They assessed any observed relationships between these creative activities and personality:

> Both the statistical analyses and the case studies indicate that children's use of color, line, form and space, can give distinctive insights into personality. Color has been found to give the clearest insights into the child's emotional life . . . . children who emphasize color tend to have strong emotional orientation. Specific color preferences and specific patterns of color placement give clues to the emotional make-up of the child. Our data support the view that red is the most emotionally toned of all the colors. From a developmental standpoint, red is a preferred color during the early preschool years, when children are naturally functioning on an impulsive level. Interest in red decreases and interest in the cooler colors increases as children outgrow the impulsive stage and grow into the stage of reasoning and of greater emotional control.

One child in this study who went through cycles of being emotionally disturbed because of specific situations within her family, and then of being happily adjusted and self-controlled when the disturbing situations had cleared, showed alternation between red-yellow-orange masses and blue or otherwise cooler colored forms and representations. The warm masses paralleled emotionally disturbed periods. The forms and lines in cooler colors paralleled periods of happy adjustment and of constructive relationships.

Emphasis on red has been found to be associated with either of two extremes: (a) feelings of affection and love; (b) feelings of aggression and hate.

Aileen's emphasis on red seemed related to a craving for affection and love. Other examples of the relation of red to love and affection or to aggression and hate appeared when we singled out the one or two red paintings in a series otherwise characterized by cool colors, and when we noted what happened to the children on those particular days to make them turn to red. In one series we found that the only red painting was done by a rejected, neglected child who usually painted in sombre colors in keeping with her predominantly dejected feelings. The one red painting occurred on a day when this child was receiving an undue amount of affection and attention . . . .

While emphasis on red seems related to strong emotional drives, emphasis on blue seems more often associated with drives toward control. Children frequently select blue as they turn away from mass and begin to work with more effort toward control in line and form. Another interesting observation is that many children who come from particularly high-standard homes, i.e., homes geared to adults rather than children, will turn to blue after an absence from school when they have been home, and gradually work away from blue as they again adjust to school and begin to function more freely and at the more impulsive level natural for children of their age . . . .

Generalized trends have also been suggested by the children's use of other colors. Green, like blue, tends to be used by children who are functioning on a relatively controlled level and show few unusually strong emotional reactions. However, children who emphasize blue may give evidence of very strong underlying emotions which they have redirected, i.e., sublimated, whereas those who emphasize green often lack all evidences of a strong underlying emotional core.

Many other experiments and studies using color as the controlling or determining factor have been made. Out of the observation by a psychiatrist that most children draw apple trees (trees with a red fruit) when asked to draw fruit trees came the famous fruit tree experiments by Adler.[6] In this cross-cultural study, the directions stated: "Draw or paint a picture— any scene, in color—with a fruit tree in it." A total of 2,906 schoolchildren of both sexes were tested in thirteen countries, including some in which apple trees are nonexistent (the tropics) or not native (South America and the Near East). The results supported the observation of apple tree popularity. Apple trees were drawn more frequently than the next six groups of trees combined. Even in those countries where the red fruit was not first choice, it was always among the three highest frequencies in all thirteen countries, something that no other category of trees showed.

A variation on this experiment by the same investigator measured the relationship between available colors and projected imagery by dividing the test sample into four groups: one had all colors to work with; another had red, blue, and yellow; another had green, brown, and orange; a fourth had only a monochrome pencil or pen. The results showed that in the green-brown-orange group, the majority of children pictured an orange tree, but the other groups showed a preponderance of apple trees regardless of their colors.

Using paper geometric figures in primary and secondary colors, first-grade children identified black, brown, yellow, green, red, blue, gray, lilac, orange, and beige—in that order. The children encountered some difficulty in distinguishing between the light and dark shades of color and often interchanged them. Girls displayed better skills in handling colors than boys did.

The "selection of colors" studies have shown that children tend to choose preferred colors more quickly than they do nonpreferred colors; thus, blue, red, and green are preferred to orange, yellow, and violet by subjects aged seventeen to twenty. Older and younger children frequently tend to be influenced in the selection of a color by the object that is colored, whereas it appears that children in the eleven-to-fourteen category often choose solely on the emotional basis of color. In studies of the color preference of children where the colors are divorced from objects, the general results indicate that there is an increasing shift from the warm to the cool end of the spectrum during the long period from about three to fifteen.

Critics of these findings question the limitations of these studies to hue, and suggest that preferences might well vary if the dimensions of brightness and saturation are included and varied. In my research I have found that variations of brightness and saturation have to be carefully controlled in hue-preference assessment, lest one or both of these dimensions make a warm color appear cool, or vice versa, thus invalidating the results in terms of hue preference. However, using these variations on the hue-preference theme with children from the ages of six to seventeen, the results support the general finding of a relatively greater female preference for warm colors and male preference for cool colors. There are also indications that the childhood preference for high chroma decreases with age.

Still other studies have assayed the relationship between color preference and the spontaneous behavior of children with play objects, such as colored blocks, sticks, balls, and boxes. Observations suggest that four- to five-year-olds are still mostly in the warm color preference category. Red is the most popular color here, with second place shared about equally between blue and green.

A study by Joan Chase using the Lowenfeld Mosaic Test with children from two to sixteen suggests that position of color in the stimulus presented for assessment is an important factor influencing the choice of color.[7] For example, when blue and black tiles were placed in end positions, seven-year-olds tended to pick them more frequently. This is also true for yellow. Position appears to have no significance in the selection of white. Color contrast appears to play a role in the selection of green. Consequently, Chase concludes that in measures of color preference, position may be an important influence.

Child, Hansen, and Hornbeck studied the color preferences of children on the dimensions of hue, brightness, and saturation.[8] While the results showed a general tendency in favor of the cool colors and against the warm colors and in favor of light colors over dark colors, they also indicated a steady increase in high saturation preferences from the first grade through the fourth grade. Then, from the fifth grade through the twelfth grade, this preference for high saturation gradually but continuously declined. Differences according to sex were also apparent. In the fourth grade, girls and boys had similar saturation preferences, but by the twelfth grade, the girls chose a higher saturation level than the boys in all colors except red. Throughout the high school years, girls also showed a decrease in preference for brightness.

As age increases, both saturation and brightness become less important than hue. The authors, unlike many experimental psychologists, attribute this more sophisticated process to cognitive differentiation rather than to purely biological processes.

A comparison of how colorblind and color-normal mentally retarded children handle color-related activities in a normal classroom setting was conducted by Salvia and Shugerts.[9] The tasks involved color matching, color naming (eight colors of high saturation and eight of low saturation), and finally word-color association to measure the connotation of colors attached to words in the reading and speaking vocabularies of retarded children. The results showed no significant difference between the colorblind and the color-normal children on the word-color association test or on the color-naming or color-matching tasks. The investigators attributed these findings, at least to some degree, to the possible use of luminosity clues on the part of the colorblind and possibly to the limited number of items within a colorblind child's defective region.

H. Rudsill noted that both educators and laymen are placing greater emphasis on the use of color in textbooks, so he decided to investigate student response to color and realism.[10]

A sample of students in the first six grades was requested to indicate preference among five pictures presented in pairs in their ten possible combinations. The combinations represented differences in amount of color and degree of realism (likeliness) in the form and in the color. Specifically, these were: (1) the uncolored photograph; (2) the colored photograph; (3) the colored drawing, realistic in form and in color; (4) the outline drawing, realistic in form but outlined in color without regard for realistic effect; (5) the colored drawing, conventional in form, decorative but unrealistic in color. The results indicated that:

> (1) If two pictures are identical in all other respects, most children prefer a realistically colored one to an uncolored one.
>
> (2) If different pictures include the same subject matter and the same colors, most children prefer the one which is treated in such manner as to give the truest appearance of realism or lifelikeness.
>
> (3) If different pictures include the same subject matter, most children prefer an uncolored one that gives them an impression of reality over a colored one which does not seem to conform to reality.
>
> (4) There is an increase in unanimity of these preferences with increase in grade level up to grade four. This greater unanimity of preference of older children, as compared with younger children, is believed to be due to the former's greater capacity for discriminating reality.
>
> (5) Typical adult opinion overemphasizes the importance of color per se and underemphasizes the importance of other qualities in illustrations for children.
>
> (6) Photographs of excellent quality, both colored and uncolored, deserve much wider use than they are at present being given in illustrations for children.
>
> (7) These findings do not justify the statement of a general principle as to comparative preference

between photographs and realistic colored drawings because the samples of the two types used
in the present study were not of equal quality.
Consideration of the first four conclusions, together with children's stated reasons for choosing
certain pictures, suggests: (a) in looking at a picture, a child apparently seeks first to recognize
its content; (b) any picture (assuming a certain
content) proves satisfying to the child in proportion to its success in making that content
appear real or lifelike—whether it is colored or
uncolored is less important than the appearance
of realism; and (c) a perfect visual representation of realism includes color, and color in pictures proves satisfying to the child in proportion
to its success in increasing the impression of
realism or lifelikeness.

Using restricted colors as in the previously mentioned
study, a replication of the "fruit-tree experiment" with mentally
retarded children showed that these children respond in a similar manner to normal children, albeit less strongly with orange
trees in the orange color group. Nevertheless, the overall hierarchical rankings were similar for both groups. The investigator
of both of the fruit-tree experiments reported here, concluded
that the differences in performance between the retardates
and normally intelligent children in this experiment may be
attributable to a deficiency in associative imagination of the
former group and that the retarded child may be slow in both
the attentional phase (notice of the orange color) and the associative phase (an orange tree).[11]

It has been assumed that the mentally retarded have the
same incidence and the same male ratio for colorblindness that
is found in the normal population, but recent studies have
shown a higher rate of colorblindness in the mentally retarded

and an almost equal number of colorblind male and female retardates. Although there are various estimates of the prevalence of colorblindness in the normal population, the general estimate is 12.5 percent of the male population, whereas studies have estimated that as high as one in five educable mentally retarded children are deficient in color vision. Colorblindness is characterized by two different forms: monochromatism and dichromatism; the former is the inability to differentiate among various hues and saturation, though brightness perception is unaffected; in the latter, the individual can perceive only two of the three basic hues—red, green, and blue. Colorblindness is inherited, the mother being the "carrier."

Areas of most concern to this group are the increasing use of visual aids in the classroom, the effect of the lack of, or diminished, color experience on emotional development and expression, and the effect of color vision on color association. There are no reported studies on the two former categories. Reported studies on the relationship between color vision and color association are almost equally divided between those who report that color vision is imparted independent of color association and those who report that the mentally retarded child with normal color vision makes color-word association more in agreement with the word association of his teachers than the color-defective mentally retarded child does. One could hardly conclude that the lack of color vision is not an added handicap on a group that already has attentional associative problems. Consequently, it can only be said that additional research is essential, along with color testing programs in the school system for the mentally retarded child.

Normal infants show a preference for a schematic representation of the human face to other visual stimuli; retardates with a mental age of less than one year showed the same preference on initial presentation; however, upon later presentation with the use of color as a conditioning stimulus, the retardates responded preferentially to the color stimulus.

Tests of designs have been shown to be a better measure than tests of color to differentiate brain-damaged children from non-brain-damaged children.

The Pfister Color Pyramid Test was given to evaluate the color preferences of feeble-minded grade school children; it was found that between the ages of six and thirteen there was little variation in color combination preferences, though a striking preference was noted for red as well as a negative correlation between red and intellectual functioning.

Color-form perception measures of juvenile delinquents have consistently shown them to be a color-dominant group. These findings are in keeping with other personality measures of this group, which have found the delinquents to be controlled by their impulses and weak in ego strength.

There is a considerable body of literature on color as a secondary cue in learning. Using the paired-associate technique, these studies have generally concentrated on color-form preference and on color as a contextual cue. Using paired-association techniques, such as words presented on cards of different colors, colored sketches in association with words, lists of similar words or dissimilar words on colored cards with either no color cues or similar color cues on transfer trials, certain overall conclusions can be drawn, although the results are mixed. Specifically, two cues are better than one and a color cue gives the subject the freedom to choose the stimulus cue of his choice (color or form), and color as a secondary learning cue does not facilitate learning on easy tasks.

Color as a secondary learning and matching cue in pre-school and for children up to about the age of twelve seems to be of most benefit to the bright child and the good reader. The overt pleasure of working with colors seems to serve as a motivational device and on that basis alone has been recommended.

Two of the most ambitious and sophisticated color cue projects are the Color Phonics System, by Bannatyne,[12] and Words in Color by Gattegno.[13]

Although these two systems differ in detail, they are similar in principle. Color is not used in either system as a secondary cue; rather it is a salient feature of the technique. One basic goal is to smooth out the irregularity of the English language by sound and symbol; for example, in the Color Phonics System, consonants and the two consonant combinations *ph* and *qu* are printed in color on a white background. Two letters with the same sound—for example, *s* and *c*—are printed with a different colored stripe running through the middle of the white letter. The letters are coded so that once the principle of the coding is learned, the child immediately recognizes each sound. This system was designed for the child with reading difficulty, whereas Words in Color was designed primarily for the normal child.

Words in Color utilizes color and sound under the assumption that the child who is learning to read has been listening and speaking the language for several years. The color approach can be especially helpful in English, where one sound may be spelled several different ways. Thus, in one sentence like the following, the italicized letters may all be in magenta to indicate that they all produce the same *e* sound. Dr*ea*ming p*eo*ple bel*ie*ve in s*ee*ing k*ey* pol*i*cemen rec*ei*ve s*e*crets. To indicate that many letters produce different sounds in different words, the italicized letters in the following sentence would have different colors according to the different pronunciations: Gr*ea*t m*ea*n ov*er*bearing *ea*rls f*ea*r h*ea*ven h*ea*rtily.

C. W. Crannell found that, upon exposure to associated

pictures of the decorative sticker variety, four groups of college students learned to produce letters of the alphabet or numerals or simple words.[14] Crannell made up his four groups by assigning two methods of learning (whole and part) and two types of pictures (in full color and in black and white) to subjects on a random basis. Neither method nor code type was found to affect the number of trials taken in original learning, nor the amount of recall after three weeks without intervening practice. The materials tended to be unusually easy to learn and to retain, and it is suggested that when this is true, little is to be gained by the use of color in the stimulus pattern.

In a recent study, Krause and Thomas worked with children from preprimary through third grade to determine whether or not there was a direct relationship between the degree of color vision disability and the perception of illustrated contextual cues, and the degree of importance of the colored contextual cues.[15] They administered four basic reading series and determined how many discriminations between colors were necessary to perceive the form of illustrated contextual cues. They found that: (1) the most common color cue discrimination was a red figure on a green background; (2) at least one primary color was in most figure-ground relationships; (3) green was the most frequent background color; and (4) "the use of color contextual cues increased in frequency as the grade level of the reader advances," through third grade. Consequently, they recommend that children with color vision difficulty be identified early so that remedial aids can be introduced at the earliest possible time.

Goldfarb and Klopfer, by the administration of Rorschach records, studied eight boys and seven girls ranging in age from ten to fourteen, with a mean of twelve years and two months, who had been in institutions since infancy.[16] The results showed that these children tended to give the pure color response with the unbalanced ratio or sum weight of form-color and color greater than form-color weight. They concluded that:

> the institution group thus shows deficiencies in rational control, in the more abstract forms of thinking, in drive for intellectual and social attainment, and in emotional maturity. In a group with such psychological tendencies, one would, of course, expect problems involving restlessness, inability to concentrate, and poor adjustment . . . all of the above listed Rorschach trends among the institution children are associated with an air of passivity. In other words, the children of this group give little of themselves, though superficially they are adjusting to reality requirements.

There appears to be some contradiction between a description of this group as restless and lacking in rational control in the first instance and "passivity" in the second.

An unbalanced color-form and color response ratio is traditionally interpreted as a reflection of an orientation that is impulsive, actively negativistic, willful, and excitable. Fortier's interpretation of this ratio in relation to this particular population is instructive here.[17]

> What this ratio actually seems to suggest here is a greater inclination to be moved and swayed by the environmental configuration in which the children find themselves. It suggests a more undifferentiated emotional approach to the environment, possibly a rather diffuse emotional reaction towards everyone with whom the children come into contact. Such behavior would logically follow from the nature of the institu-

tions in which the children find themselves forced to live. Their behavior is in virtually every respect governed by more or less impersonal rules and regulations. Their relations with adults are limited simply because there are so few adults in the institutions that personal contact is quite difficult. The suggestion follows naturally that for one to have sufficient intellectual control of affectivity one must have the opportunity to learn and develop this capacity. It is probable, then, that the nature of one's affective life is dependent, above native endowment, perhaps, upon the ability and opportunity to learn.

Rorschach defined a color response as one motivated by "not only the form of the blots, but also the color or the color alone . . . ."[18] Three kinds of color responses are differentiated: (1) the FC (form-color) answer is one in which the emphasis is on the form first, then the color; (2) the CF responses emphasize first color, then form; and (3) the C response is motivated solely by color—form has no bearing whatsoever. His Sum C, or composite score, is computed by weighing FC .5, CF 1.0, and C 1.5. The most frequent score for normal adults is 3FC, 1CF, and 0C. In an earlier study, Monnier stated that the normal, well-adjusted adult should give approximately 18 percent color responses out of a maximum of forty responses.[19] In a later revision, he stated that a normal protocol should contain 14 percent color responses, 73 percent form responses, and 13 percent movement responses.[20]

Marked emotionality has traditionally been one of the most frequent psychological characteristics associated with delinquents; however, studies using Rorschach reports have tended to refute this widespread theory. A highly rigid, stereotyped orientation appears to be a more adequate description of the delinquents' lifestyle. A comparison of a study done by Endacott[21] of two delinquent boys with an average age of fourteen showed a greater restriction in the use of color (with a lower FC and lower CF) than a study done by Hertz and Baker[22] with a sample of nondelinquent, high-average intelligence, high socioeconomic status group of boys of the same age level. In fact, the latter sample showed a sum C weight of one to one and one-half points higher than did the delinquent group. Boynton and Wadsworth showed essentially the same results with a comparison of the Rorschach protocols of a group of delinquents and of a group of girls who attended a public high school in the favored portion of a city.[23] Specifically, the delinquent group scored lower than the advanced group on all measures of color responses, with the critical impulsivity ratio of CF + C (which is traditionally associated with delinquent behavior) more in favor of the latter than the former group.

The conflict here, between the long-held theories of emotionality as the major ingredient in delinquent behavior and the unexpected low C scores, has raised questions regarding personality aberration as a factor in delinquent behavior. I do not find it unusual that delinquents often show low color scores on the Rorschach and that they often show normal color-form responses that indicate a realistic approach to the environment. In fact, realistic is the key word in describing the delinquent. It appears that many of these children tend to see life as starkly realistic, free of the frosting that most people, consciously or unconsciously, put on it to make it palatable. They either do not respect what they see or are unable to deal effectively with the fact-fiction aspects of reality, and so they move against society rather than with it. There is a high degree of consistency between the delinquent's behavior and his perceived reality.

In his thorough and excellent review and analysis of the Rorschach responses of various groups, Fortier[24] used the

Phillips and Stromberg[25] comparative study of the finger painting of a group of delinquents and a group of "average" high
school youths when he found the Rorschach responses of the
aberrant group not in keeping with the traditional interpretation of the inkblots. Fortier summarized the results of the Phillips and Stromberg study:

> While a number of significant differences are
> reported in their study, only one need be discussed
> here. Thirty-six percent of the high school group
> used only one color on the first performance.
> Sixty-four percent of the delinquents used only
> one color on the first performance. This difference
> is not quite significant at the .05 level. However,
> on the second performance, 4 percent of the high
> school students used only one color. The result
> of this comparison is highly significant statis-
> tically. If it can be assumed that one's handling
> of color is indicative of his affective life, both the
> non-delinquent and the delinquent to a greater
> degree might here be showing a certain amount
> of shock when confronted with a new—and per-
> haps affective—situation, and thus respond in a
> somewhat stereotyped manner. However, the non-
> delinquent shows a considerable degree of recov-
> erability and a capacity for a wide variety of
> response. The delinquent, on the other hand,
> continues to show a stereotyped reaction. When
> one recalls a deduction made from the evidence
> reviewed concerning institutionalized children,
> it is possible that the environment in which
> delinquents live does not make it possible for
> them to learn a variety of emotional reactions.
> Thus, while it may not be any fundamental lack
> of capacity for emotional rapport or ego control

of affect which contributes to their antisocial behavior, it may be an inability of the delinquents to vary their emotional response. This suggestion accords with the reduced use of color in general on the Rorschach test and the reduced use of CF by delinquents.

The extensive body of literature on enuretic children consistently portrays them as infantile and nonconformist and as having high affective energy. They also tend to move against the world, to be aggressive, and to lack the self-control essential to consistent performance in academic tasks and in dealing with others. Their Rorschach protocols tend to have high color totals, an overabundance of color-form and uncontrolled color responses.

Fortier questions the wisdom of labeling the child who makes unbalanced color responses as infantile; he feels that a description of the dynamics of the dysfunction is a more valid approach.[26] He suggests that the enuretic child manifesting this kind of color response is making a diffuse reaction to environmental stimuli; hence the child is lacking in ego control, and in turn these two factors contribute to the symptom.

Studies of the Rorschach responses of the hysteric show a predominance of CF and C responses over FC, which indicates great susceptibility to environmental influence and a minimization of active control of this influence.

Although epileptics give fewer color responses than do normals on the Rorschach, their responses are unbalanced in favor of CF and C, thus suggesting that the epileptic has limited emotional communication with the environment and that such communication, as does exist, is diffuse, undifferentiated, and coarse.

Individuals in whom there has been actual destruction of brain tissue—a group referred to as organics—are generally found to be extratensive, with CF and C responses predominant over FC. It is not infrequent that these individuals give color names. Color naming in this group can be either the adoption of a highly concrete, ineffective attitude or a reflection of the inability to effectively handle affective situations. Other tests of organics have shown a strong tendency toward perseverance and concreteness. Consequently, the former conclusion as regards Rorschach responses seems to be all the more valid.

The studies considered in this chapter indicate in general that, as the child matures into the young adult, the emotional and intellectual sides of his personality differentiate. In most cases, the early dominance of the emotional side is modified and finally surpassed by the intellect. Most cultures regard this as a desirable sequence of events and reward youngsters who tread this well-worn path. A child who, for instance, retains his color-dominance long after the "normal" time of switchover to form-dominance is regarded as infantile even if he has a realistic response to form. These color-oriented youngsters are subjected to academic and cultural enrichment programs as a means of changing their orientation. Yet some recent studies of creativity suggest that the color-oriented child is the one who is more likely to emerge as an adult who is more artistic, more creative, more innovative than the form-dominant person, whose pursuits tend to deal with facts, figures, details, and the like. One of the ingredients of creative ability seems to be naïveté (which some might call immaturity), the facility to be more or less free of the traditional modes of doing things and to see new possibilities, new relationships, unheard-of combinations.

Thus, the possibility suggests itself that the color-form instruments of measure may be able to point out potential creativity. At the least, the hypothesis can be made that creativity has its foundation in an emotionally oriented personality structure. If further studies support this theory, the color-oriented child not only should be permitted to retain his orientation but also should be encouraged and helped rather than remade in the image of the form-dominant child.

Of course, there are degrees of ability and orientation. Some abnormal children have such a high color dominance that there is simply no structure or self-discipline available for adequate form control. These children need help in this area, just as perhaps the extreme form-dominant youngster might benefit from a program that encourages self-expression, spontaneity, and the freedom to make mistakes without censure.

The delinquent child, for example, has been diagnosed as one who is controlled by his id at the expense of the socially controlled ego. He acts impulsively, free from any normal feelings of guilt or other social, learned restraint. This Freudian analysis is in complete accord with the color-form theory that equates the id with color and the ego with form. And the color-form index offers a simple, quick, straightforward measure of this orientation compared with the Freudian techniques, which can be time consuming and highly complicated in both diagnosis and treatment.

Whether normal, subnormal, or supranormal, children will continue to be ideal subjects for tests and inventories that measure the influence of culture and learning. Although there is an increasing emphasis on inherited characteristics, especially in individual behavior, children as a whole are still perceived pretty much in Rousseau's "blank tablet" frame of reference.

3/Culture and color

As was noted in the last chapter, the color responses of young people are valuable to investigators in that the younger the child, the freer he is from the influences of learning, experience, and culture. But even in children cultural differences are apparent. Many studies that have been made of both adults and children reveal the disparities among various peoples' responses to colors. The differences and likenesses in color preferences between and across groups have also been assessed with the ultimate goal of perhaps developing a culture-free test that could be used to assess individual differences around the world.

Martin Lindauer analyzed the colors of the flags of the world as a reflection of color preferences within the social-psychological context of traditions and aspirations.[1] The 139 independent nations of the world were broken down into six major geographic areas—Africa, Asia, Europe, Latin America, the Middle East, and other (including the U.S.A.). The average flag had 2.14 colors; in 97 percent of these flags the colors used were red, blue, green, and yellow, in that order. Red appeared in 38 percent of the flags, blue in 22 percent, green in 19 percent, and yellow in 18 percent. White was used in 78 percent of 107 flags. There were forty-seven flags in which one color covered a greater area than any other color. In 49 percent of those flags, the dominant color was red. The proportionate use of red, blue, and yellow in the flags did not significantly vary according to geographic area. However, a disproportionate use of color green was noted in African flags.

The investigator stated that other studies have shown that color preferences do vary among different geographic groups, and the fact that these preferences are not reflected in flag color selections may be attributed to the possibility of "the ad hoc treatment of flag data . . . and also from examining isolated colors out of context. There also appears to be a universality of color meaning as relating to flags." He concluded that, although he ran the risk of appearing chauvinistic, the ideal flag, based on these findings, would be very close to "Old Glory."

Knapp's data on color preference as related to n achievement formed the basis for a later study of the colors of the American state flags.[2] His data revealed a relationship between a preference for somber blues and greens and high scores in the standard psychological measure, n achievement, and between a preference for reds and yellows and low n achievement. (See page 65.) He drew the following historical parallel:

> The Puritans, imbued with very strong achievement motivation, eschewed all but the somberest of dress and ornament, imposing fines for the wearing of bright colors, destroyed the stained glass windows in churches, and cultivated unconditional austerity in dress and decor. They stand in dramatic contrast to the Cavaliers with their feudal and chivalric traditions of ascribed status, colorful dress, and fondness for indulgent living.

Knapp led McClelland[3] to hypothesize that the flags of the U.S. would reflect both achievement motive and philosophical orientation, because the state flags were adopted at a time when religious, economic, and philosophical differences were highly accented. Specifically, the flags of the northern states would reflect the Puritan influences with blues and greens, and those of the southern states would reflect the reds and yellows of Cavalier influence. An analysis of the colors of the state flags supported McClelland's hypothesis in terms of color distribution. Blue-green characterizes 91 percent of twenty-one northern flags; of the southern flags that are classifiable in terms of specific color direction, 60 percent are predominantly red-yellow. The difference between the two is statistically significant. In terms of the achievement motive, the author states that:

> It tends to confirm the belief that high n achievement is associated with preference for blues and greens over reds and yellows because of various kinds of indirect evidence that n achievement has been higher in the North than in the South—the greater economic development in the North, its closer association with the kind of radical Protestantism that was associated with high n achievement—and the presence of household slaves in the South which should lower n achievement in the children they rear.

Lindauer, however, did not find a high and a low n achievement color division between the flags of the world.[4] Symbolically used throughout history, colors appear to have been a unifying force rather than a reflection of differences, so perhaps it is on this basis that flags are designed, consciously or unconsciously.

Some of the early writers on color have flatly stated that

color preferences are almost identical for all races, creeds, and sexes and that the universally admired colors are blue and red. Although recent research is at times contradictory, it suggests that there is no world-wide order of color preferences, but there is the fact that different cultures have different attitudes toward various colors.

Chongourian inventoried the color preferences of college students from the United States, Iran, Lebanon, and Kuwait among eight colors roughly within the spectrum range using Ostwald color notations.[5] His findings indicate that red and blue had the highest preference value only for Americans. (Perhaps this extension of our color preferences to all races and creeds reflects American authoritarian attitudes, in which it is assumed that whatever America likes, everyone else should like.) On the contrary, red and blue had the lowest ranking in Kuwait. Blue-green, the most preferred color in Iran and Kuwait, was the least preferred of the eight colors among the Americans. Orange and yellow-green fluctuate within the middle range of the eight-step ranking scale. Green was consistently rated high by all four nationalities. The combined color preferences for all groups indicate that blue is significantly preferred by men and not preferred by women. Blue-green, however, was significantly preferred by the women in this study, although it should be noted that American women have indicated a preference for red on other surveys. It is interesting to point out that women's preference for red was unsettling to Lindauer, when he recalled the prominence of red in most flags, and "the image of the flag as a rallying point in most battles." The finding would not have unsettled Margaret Mead, the noted anthropologist, who has made a statement to the effect that women should not be permitted to engage in warfare because they are so fierce that every battle would become a massacre.

Chongourian conducted another study of American and Lebanese students, male and female, at different levels of education.[6] The combined results show that green had a higher preference order at the later developmental stage than at the earlier stages—the significance of green here is in keeping with his previously discussed research. The later developmental stages are also characterized by a preference for blue and red and a nonpreference for blue-green, yellow, and purple. The most noteworthy finding of this survey was that by the age of five, American children demonstrate a preference for red, whereas Lebanese children of this age level have no color preferences that differ significantly from chance.

For my informal survey of 200 Puerto Rican adults, men and women, I used the following Ostwald color notations: orange, yellow, green, green-blue (turquoise), blue, purple, and red. Turquoise was included on the advice of a Venezuelan interior designer, who predicted that it would receive a high rating and that any array of color stimuli that did not include turquoise would not be a fair sample of colors for this particular population. The results showed that turquoise and blue were preferred equally, with red in second position. In considering these findings, one should keep in mind that these results were obtained under a survey-type situation as opposed to a more formal testing situation.

The findings of most of the above studies suggest that there can be no culture-free instruments of color testing capable of assaying individual differences, unless separate norms for males and females in each culture in which the test was to be used were established.

Measures of color preferences tend to be narrow in scope, often one-dimensional; that is, a subject has a favorite color, and has neutral or mixed feelings about other colors. The introduction of the Semantic Differential (SD) by Osgood and associates at the University of Illinois permitted a wider range of affective responses to color studies.[7] However, color preference appears to have its own unique facets, its own mystique. Color preference is subjective compared to the objective rating of the SD.[8]

Since the Semantic Differential is a relatively effective measuring instrument of color preference, it seems logical at this point to explain it in some detail. It can provide objective, quantified measurements of connotative (expressive) meaning by presenting an individual with a concept and a set of bipolar adjectival scales with which to differentiate the concept. The adjectives are thought of as opposites, such as good-bad, and are separated by a seven point scale presented in the following manner:

good___:___:___:___:___:___:___bad

The respondent places a check mark in one of the spaces according to the direction and intensity he attributes to the stimulus being rated; the center position is neutral.

The SD is based on the theory of an unknown dimensionality, Euclidian in nature, called "semantic space." The bipolar adjectives are the extreme points on a straight line passing through the origin of this space. Several of these scales make up the different dimensions. There are three primary factors in the SD. In order of importance, they are evaluation (E), potency (P), and activity (A). E is positive to negative; P is weak to strong; A is passive to active. Each of these three factors can be thought of as one of the dimensions of a three-dimensional semantic space. The SD enables one to find the distance (D) between different concepts in semantic space. This distance is computed by first obtaining the mean of the scales representing each factor and then taking the difference between the scores of two stimuli for each factor, squaring these differences, adding up the squares, and computing the square root of the sum. The closer that two concepts lie in semantic space, the smaller is the

D measure and the closer the connotations (expressive meanings) of the compared stimuli.

As a further example, we can take nine bipolar adjective pairs from a list of fifty pairs whose factor loadings were computed by Osgood et al. Three pairs of adjectives were selected to represent each of the three factors, E, P, and A. These adjectives are presented in Table 1. Note that the first three pairs of adjectives—good-bad, beautiful-ugly, and happy-sad—all have high E factor loadings and relatively low P and A loadings. The factor means for these scales are E,.83; P,.03; and A, .03. The second three pairs of adjectives—strong-weak, heavy-light, and thick-thin—have high P factor and low E and A factor loadings: E,.08; P,.56; and A,.01. The last three pairs—fast-slow, active-passive, and hot-cold—are high in A and low in E and P: E,.04; P,.01; and A,.58. These nine scales were selected for their high loading characteristics for one of the factors and relatively low loading characteristics for the other two factors.

Table 1

Bipolar adjectives	Factor loadings		
	Evaluation	Potency	Activity
good-bad	.88	.05	.09
beautiful-ugly	.86	.09	.01
happy-sad	.76	-.11	.00
strong-weak	.19	.62	.20
heavy-light	-.36	.62	-.11
thick-thin	-.06	.44	-.06
fast-slow	.01	.00	.70
active-passive	.14	.04	.59
hot-cold	-.04	-.06	.46

The Osgood group reported that the factor variance spread on a group of English words was 34 percent of the total variance spread for evaluation, 8 percent for potency, and 6 percent for activity. Other studies that used word or verbal concepts stimuli have reported similar results; studies in this category have reported a different salience ordering of the factors. For example, the factor loadings on Tucker's study of paintings showed that the activity factor was the most salient, with 46 percent of the total variance.[9] Evaluation accounted for 17 percent, and potency accounted for 10 percent. Miron's cross-cultural study of phonetic symbolism using auditory stimuli with both Japanese and American subjects[10] showed a factor spread similar to the results obtained by Tucker.

On the basis of these findings, Tanaka et al.[11] hypothesized that the factorial composition of one class of concepts may have an ordering that is significantly different from that of another class of concepts. Abstract words and line forms were selected as the stimuli, and a factor analysis was made of each concept class, followed by an analysis across the three concept classes. Cross-cultural and cross-linguistic influences were tested by using Japanese and American subjects. Finally, the manner in which different language-culture groups utilize the same semantic concepts was investigated.

The results of this study demonstrated a cross-cultural generality in that evaluation, potency, and activity were the three most significant factors as a group. However, as class concept changed, there was a different ordering of the factor loadings. Interestingly, the same degree of change was evident in both the Japanese and the American groups. In the judgment of colors, activity was the most salient for abstract words; and potency was most salient for forms, although this was less clearly true for Americans than for Japanese on this latter factor.

By the fact that the factor loadings shifted to a·different order of significance for the three concept classes "and by the different scale compositions of the factors for different concept classes" cross-concept uniqueness was also demonstrated.

Another study using Japanese and American subjects was conducted by Oyama et al., in which the affective dimensions of color were assessed by using the Semantic Differential.[12] The results indicated that, on the activity factor, both groups found red the most exciting, or hot, color and blue or blue-purple the most calm, or cold, colors. Black, gray, and white were rated as calm. There was a decrease in the degree of excitability as the colors went from red to orange to yellow to green and finally to blue and blue-purple. This cross-cultural trend agreed with the long-established warm-versus-cold dimension of color classification.

On the evaluation factor, the Japanese rated blue-green and blue as good and orange and red-purple as bad, while the Americans rated red, yellow, green, and blue as good and orange and red-purple as bad. To explain the difference in ratings here, the investigators suggested that Americans may have a greater tendency than the Japanese to prefer primary colors.

On the potency factor, black, red, blue, and purple were rated as strong, or heavy, by both groups. There was also rating agreement by both groups that white, yellow, yellow-orange, and yellow-green are weak, or light. This cross-cultural finding was in general agreement with previous studies in which the apparent weight of colors was categorized.[13]

Correlations of the three factor loadings with the three dimensions—hue, brightness, and saturation—show that activity has a significant negative correlation with hue and a positive correlation with brightness. Hue is correlated with the Japanese evaluation factor loading; the American evaluation factor loading appears to be unrelated to any one of the three psychophysical dimensions of color. A significantly negative correlation was found between potency factors and saturation in both the Japanese and the American samples.

Williams investigated the relationship between racial attitudes and color names to test his hypothesis that the designation of racial groups by color names may influence and maintain the feelings, values, and attitudes held toward that group.[14] Measures of racial attitude toward Negroes were obtained from 96 Caucasian students on a Likert-type attitude scale and rating of the concept "Negro" on a Semantic Differential scale: 154 subjects rated Negroes on a social distance scale; and 51 subjects rated Negroes on a Woodmansee and Cook scale of attitude. The results of these instruments were correlated with the E (evaluation) scores of the race-related colors black, brown, white, red, and yellow. The color name black was significantly correlated with all of the measures of racial attitude toward Negroes; the color name brown was correlated significantly with all of the measures of racial attitude toward Negroes; the color name brown was also correlated significantly with four of the attitude scales. The color names white, red, and yellow, as rated on the evaluation scores of the Semantic Differential, did not correlate significantly with either of the measures of attitude. Thus, the investigator concluded that there is a significant relationship between skin color—as reflected in the color code names of black and brown—and attitude toward Negro people, and that racially color-coded names for this group may well be one of the determinants of prevalent racial attitudes.

Kastl and Child[15] compared the responses to color stimuli of American students of high school age to those of Vietnamese students of the same approximate grade levels. Differences in preference for cool hues varied slightly: 63 percent of Vietnamese boys and girls responded positively to cool hues, whereas 76 percent of U.S. girls and 74 percent of U.S. boys did. American girls preferred a more saturated color by 67 percent to 33 percent, while 82 percent of American boys favored saturation. With the Vietnamese, the figures were 68 percent for the boys and only 47 percent for the girls. A large sex difference was also noted in brightness: 74 percent of the Vietnamese boys preferred the lighter color, as did 58 percent of the girls. Among the Americans, 73 percent of the girls and 56 percent of the boys favored the lighter color.

Using a color-form matching test, R. Serpell investigated the relationship between preference for color or form to age, intelligence, education, sex, personality, deafness, culture, and race.[16] This study showed that:

> (1) increasing education led to greater preference for form among urban English, urban Indian, and rural Zambian children, but not among remote rural or urban Zambian children, (2) age was less directly related to form-preference than education among rural Zambian children, (3) rural and urban Zambian children prefer color more than English and Indian urban children and less than remote rural Zambian children at the same grade level. (4) Zambian university students preferred form more than illiterate Zambian adults, (5) no racial differences were found in a privileged infant-school sample.

Serpell suggests that demonstrated differences might be explained in terms of types of perceptual experiences rather than cultural differences.

Kellagham used a sample of Nigerian children between the ages of 6 and 12 to investigate preference in the use of concepts of color, form, and size.[17] The sample was divided into two groups, one described as relatively Westernized and the other as non-Westernized. The results showed that the relatively non-Westernized group preferred color more often than the relatively Westernized group. Females showed a greater preference for color than did males. Preference for color in the relatively non-Westernized group varied somewhat from age to age; there was no consistent trend. The relatively Westernized group resembled the European children in the increase of form preference and decrease of color preference with age. This test seems to show that cultural factors have an influence on preference.

Color is preferred more frequently than size by both groups on color-size choices by both groups. The relatively non-Westernized group preferred color more than did the relatively Westernized group. The males contributed more to the size preference than did the females.

Using male elementary school students and illiterate men in Northeastern Liberia, Irwin and McLaughlin investigated the relationship between schooling, preference, and ability in sorting by color, number, and form.[18] They found that both the schooled and unschooled subjects preferred color to form. These findings are in general agreement with other studies of equivalent groups using African subjects. Number was also preferred to form by both groups and was even slightly preferred to color. The investigators explain that number preference suggests that it is not the uniqueness of color that accounts for its dominance but perhaps a perceptual immediacy or unidimensionality common to both color and number configuration. Since preference was not a factor in the ability to sort by color, number, and shape, the failure to sort by form in other studies can not be attributed entirely to color preferences. The failure of African subjects to group by form, according to these investigators, is attributable not to a developmental lag in abstraction abilities, as has been hypothesized by other investigators, but rather "appears to be due to little interest among Africans in form complex classifications (e.g., by shape or function) of objects." Schooling also seems to be a critical factor in form sorting; however, it does not significantly increase form preference.

Studies made fifteen years ago of the skin color preferences of Negro children, six and seven years of age, showed that these children tended to reject their race; somewhat older children showed less rejection, although there was still overall rejection of the skin color brown by both groups. Recent studies, on the other hand, reveal a striking shift by Negro students to a preference for their own skin color.[19] This supports the remark by Kenneth Clark: "As children develop an awareness of racial differences of their racial identities, they also develop an awareness and acceptance of the prevailing social attitudes and values toward race and skin color."[20]

A recent study of Glick investigated the possible effects of a teacher's skin color upon student test performance under experimental conditions.[21] Using a group of black male students, a black and a white teacher, and multiethnic materials, he did not find any differences in test performance between those students exposed to either teacher. Neither did he note a measurable difference between the use of multiethnic teaching materials and the use of traditional materials.

The pervasive use of white to symbolize positive evaluation and black to symbolize negative evaluation suggests that there is considerable cross-cultural generality in the connotative meanings of colors and color names. Although many investigators have studied the symbolic meaning of color across cultures, some of the most ambitious research has been conducted by Williams et al, specifically their study of North American Caucasians and Negroes, Germans, Danes, Chinese, and East Indians. The subjects were all college students, and the Semantic Differential was the test instrument. An examination of the evaluation scale reveals a high degree of similarity across groups. White, yellow, red, brown, and black were ranked from positive to negative in that order by North American Caucasians. The North American Negroes, Chinese, and East Indians all ranked them in the same order but they showed little difference between yellow, red, and brown. The Danes showed a slightly more positive shift for red than yellow, with black and brown similarly rated. The German students rated red second to white; they gave yellow and black the same rating, and they rated brown most negatively of all. While small differences did seem to exist, white consistently received the highest positive rating, and brown and black received the most negative rating.

On the potency factor, the intercorrelations show that the East Indians rated white stronger and brown weaker than did the other groups. However, there was general agreement among the groups on yellow and white as weak, and red and black as strong.

There were no deviant individual scores for the activity factor, and the overall ratings classified gray as most passive and brown and black as relatively passive. Red was generally rated as the most active and white and yellow relatively so.

In order to assess the influence of language on the similarity of ratings, the investigators statistically analyzed the data according to English language groups and other language groups. No relationship was found between the scale ratings of color and language. The data was subjected to further analysis by dividing the groups into a Caucasian group (North American, German, and Danish), and a non-Caucasian group (North American Negro, Chinese, and East Indian) to determine whether or not the similarities within groups might be greater than the similarities among groups. No relationship was found between either of these variables and ratings of color.

Further studies by Williams et al. and other scientific investigators to determine the process by which color names acquire symbolic meanings across cultures, suggest that associative learning and the physical characteristics of color may, at least in part, account for this phenomenon.

Most cultures are filled with examples of the use of black to symbolize evil and wickedness and white to symbolize goodness and purity. From the dawn of literature, writers have attached emotional meaning to colors. An analysis of a writer's use of color symbolism reveals how he looks out at the world. "Red herring," "white lie," "black sheep," and "purple prose" are common terms. Early childhood experiences of fears of darkness, black (dirty) face and hands and the rewards of cleaning them are universal experiences.

As an explanation of the results obtained on the potency and activity scales of the Semantic Differential with color name rating, Williams et al. speculated that the potency connotations may well be related to the saturation dimension of color. Specifically, yellow, gray, and white are low in saturation and are consequently rated weak, whereas purple, brown, red, and black are heavily saturated and are rated strong. The degree of activity rating for a color name appears to be a function of wavelength, as seen in the increasing activity ratings of purple, blue, green, orange, yellow, and red.

Since racial groups are color coded, Caucasians being called "white," Negroes "black," Indians "red," Chinese "yellow," and since color naming carries specific connotations, it is suggested that the color coding of racial groups influences the way in which these groups are perceived and reacted to. This possible link has been studied by numerous investigators. Williams and Renninger sought to determine the age period during which the concepts of black as bad and white as good were formed, and to relate these to the formation of racial attitudes.[22] Morland found that the rate at which Caucasian children recognized individuals by race increased sharply between the ages of three and five, with 80 percent of five-year-olds being able quite consistently to paint "colored" and "white" persons.[23] He also noted that a majority of Caucasian children between ages three to five expressed a preference for light-skinned playmates, and this preference remained stable.[24] Williams and Renninger's study suggested that color-meaning concepts were being learned by their Caucasian sample during the third, fourth, and fifth years. The period during which the preschool child is learning the evaluative meaning of black as bad and white as good is also the period in which race awareness is developing, so the investigators speculated upon the possible implications of the color-meaning concept in the childhood origins of anti-Negro prejudice. One dramatic example of the black-bad, white-good learning situations to which children are exposed is a teaching aid called *The Wordless Book* in which each of its five colored pages represents a particular religious concept, with the black page representing sin and the white page representing the absence of sin.

The fact that Negro and white adults attribute essentially the same connotative values to the color words black and white suggests that these terms are culturally determined and that the preschool Negro child acquires a distorted self-image from the same source.

In view of these findings, the recent trend among Negroes to refer to themselves as "blacks" would seem to be a negative factor in the establishment of accurate racial evaluation. A study I conducted several years ago revealed that there was a small shift to a more positive direction (but still negative) in the rating of black than in studies of previous years. However, the emphasis upon racial color coding seems to have little of value to offer to any racial group, and the habit of doing so appeared to be diminishing until Negroes revived it a few years ago.

In order to avoid offending anyone in another country,

through the use of a color or symbol that was prohibited, disapproved of, or unpopular for cultural, religious, or other reasons, Winick interviewed citizens, exporters, and consular and diplomatic officials of various foreign countries.[25] His four-page, open-ended questionnaire interview included questions of a critical incident nature in which the subject was asked to recall, if possible, an incident in which the use of a disapproved color or symbol had created an unpleasant situation. For a country to be included in the finished study, unanimous agreement among the three exporters and the two diplomatic or consular officials representing each country was necessary; also, thirty of the thirty-five informants for each country had to include the particular color or symbol that was unpopular. The results were presented by continent, and in general showed that there appears to be a preference for the familiar. Therein apparently lies a strong reinforcement of self-perception, as well as national identification.

Studies of the color preferences of children in Israel, Spain, China, and North America show some slight differences.[26] Kindergarten children in Israel indicated red as the most preferred color, and chose blue second and yellow third. In Madrid, schoolchildren ranging in age from approximately five years to fourteen years indicated a preference order of blue (most often preferred), then yellow, red, and green. Color preferences tended to vary with form and size; with these two factors held constant, the above colors were selected. The order of color preference for Chinese students has been found to be white, blue, red, yellow, green, black, orange, violet, and gray.

Winick noted that black is the most unpopular color among the African nations on which he obtained data, suggesting that weather, symbolism, and association may play a role in this disapproval. Specifically, white clothes are frequently worn in hot weather. Black has a symbolic meaning in the area of darkness and corruption and an associative meaning in the area of death. The widespread disapproval of black on the Asian continent appears to be based on some of the same reasons. In addition, Hindus and Buddhists regard black as *Tamas*—reference to persons who have low moral and intellectual capacity or who have become demons.

Purple, the traditional color of mourning among many peoples, meets disapproval in six Asian countries. Iran, a predominantly Arab state, disapproves of gold and yellow, while countries like India, Ceylon, Burma, Cambodia, and Laos, which are composed predominantly of Hindus and Buddhists, exhibit a preference for gold and yellow. Green is not disapproved of in any Arab country, and it is preferred over all other colors in Iran, Iraq, Pakistan, Indonesia, the Sudan, and Jordan.

The authors of the study told the story of the exporter who planned to use a reproduction of Venus de Milo on a package to be sent to an Arab country. He changed his mind, however, when he discovered that the chopping off of hands is a traditional punishment in Arab areas. Then, of course, there is the religiously based prohibition on the reproduction of any image of man or beast.

Black is unpopular in Australia, along with the red rising sun, which is probably associated with Japan in World War II.

Eleven of the eighteen European countries on which Winick obtained sufficient data to include in the study disapprove of black, seven disapprove of the swastika, and two disapprove of the hammer and sickle, the Russian symbol. Noting that there are political overtones in some of these rejections, mention is made of the contradiction between the rejection of the Nazi swastika but not of the fasces, wreath, and ax of Italian fascism. The fact no European country expressed disapproval of the color gold, although rejections for it are found in Latin America and Asia, is attributable possibly to the way in which gold is used in money and jewelry in Europe.

Three of the seven North and Central American countries surveyed disapprove of black and two reject violet. Black is disapproved of in two of the four South American countries on which sufficient data was obtained for inclusion in this study. Although brown and gray are not culturally disapproved of and do find some acceptance for uses in the home, they are not favored for wearing apparel because of "a tendency to heighten muddiness and sallowness of the skin."

Blue is the only color that in itself is not disapproved. Politics appear to lie at the root of many color disapprovals—some people do not want the colors of their national flag used in anything except the flag. Some countries reject the colors used by previous rulers or enemies in battle.

Religion is another major factor in the rejection of colors and objects. Colors associated with mourning are rejected for popular usage. Asian countries disapprove of the sign of the cross, but Christian countries do not. Arab nations disapprove of representations of Mohammed as well as of anything living. Pictures of the cow and the monkey are acceptable in India but are disapproved of by Arabs.

Climate also plays a role in rejected colors. Light-colored clothing is preferred in hot climates, dark-colored in cold climates. Dark clothes are preferred, in general, by those living on plains and deserts as against those living in hilly areas.

It is apparent from data presented and analyzed in this chapter that there are definite cultural and racial differences in the way people look at, and receive impressions of, various colors. There are also certain seemingly universal likes and dislikes, which perhaps indicate an innate or biologically mandated response to various colors in people. This concept will be used in the last chapter of the book. The intelligent student of color will do well to be alert to the different ways that the peoples of the world see color, since this subject has implications beyond simply the preferences of a particular racial or national group.

4/Color and personality

Color is the most relative of all phenomena, and few people see two colors alike. One may tend to see more yellow in a red than his neighbor, for instance, even though they are looking at the same color from the same distance and angle and in the same light. The differences between individual estimates are amazingly large. The normal human eye is capable of discriminating approximately 7 million different colors, but there are only about 150 discernible wavelengths in the visible spectrum which stretches from approximately 380 to 780 mu. In turn, the average observer can name with a reasonable degree of accuracy only about 12 or 13 of these wavelengths. Kelly and Judd in the 1950s prepared a dictionary of over 5 thousand different color names, but since color names are restricted only by man's need and ingenuity, each year new ones are invented.[1]

Color names in popular usage are made up of two parts, generally, the basic color name and a modifier—for example, shocking pink. Many of these names have little meaning for the average person. Chapanis conducted a study in which he found that there are probably only about 52 to 53 usable color names for all color space.[2] (Color space is commonly referred to as all possible variations on the three dimensions of color—hue, brightness, and saturation.)

Numerous studies have been made of the color preferences of North American men and women. When brightness and saturation are held the same for all colors, people have shown a preference for hues of shorter wavelength; that is, the blues and greens are preferred to the yellows, reds, and oranges. Specifically, the order of preference across the spectrum is:

Blue
Red
Green
Violet
Orange
Yellow

Guilford and Smith attribute this "community of color preferences among individuals" to biological factors.[3] Other investigations have emphasized the role of culture, learning, experience, and genetics in color likes and dislikes. (See chapter 3.) A combination of all these factors would seem to be a more reasonable explanation. It should be noted that when a color is designated as preferred, it does not mean that one would necessarily want a preponderance of this particular color in his environment, but rather that this color has a special meaning for him in comparison with other colors. Saturated colors are preferred to unsaturated colors. Women show a slight preference for red over blue, men for blue over red. Orange is preferred to yellow by men, and yellow to orange by women. For both groups greenish-yellow is one of the least liked of the chromatic colors.

Laymen and color consultants (a general term that seems to

be applied to themselves by nonscientists and nonpsychologists) have written books on color from a so-called psychological point of view. These writings have for the most part included myth, purloined scientific works that have not always been appropriately analyzed and have often been distorted to fit the needs of the book, and speculation. Tone and color choice are among the heavy areas of interest to these writers because of the popular appeal of the subject and the possible extrapolation of these associations to a variety of practical applications.

Scientific investigations have not been without their shortcomings in this area either; too many have had ambiguous word lists, inadequate control of stimuli, or inappropriate sample size and diversity of subjects. Recent research has shown the superiority of the scaling techniques of the Osgood Semantic Differential as opposed to the all-or-nothing-at-all response measure in the adjective checklist in measuring subjective phenomena.

Using college students primarily as an index of how adults in general associate mood tone and color, numerous research projects have generally shown that red, yellow, and orange are associated with excitement, stimulation, and aggression; blue and green are associated with calm, security, and peace; black, brown, and gray are associated with melancholy, sadness, and depression; yellow is associated with cheer, gaiety, and fun; and purple is associated with dignity, royalty, and sadness. While there tends to be some overlap in colors and adjectives, general categorizations show the warm end of the spectrum (red, yellow, orange) to be exciting and stimulating, and the cool end (green and blue) to be peaceful, cool, and restful.

Guilford has said that research findings "point very strongly to a basic communality of color preferences among individuals. This communality probably rests upon biological factors, since it is hard to see how cultural factors could produce by conditioning the continuity and system that undoubtedly exist."[4] Goldstein gives specific examples of the physiological influence of color on the organism by citing the example of a woman who had a cerebellar disease and disturbance of equilibrium whose symptoms increased notably when she wore a red dress.[5] He also experimented with the relationship between body position and exposure of patients to large sheets of colored paper and found that different colors changed the position of the arms, "as a matter of fact, the whole organism had an inner or an outer orientation depending upon the color," the colors being blue and red, respectively.

Lawler and Lawler postulated that if the Guilford theory of biological determinants in color choices rests upon scientific fact, then color-mood associations found in adults would exist in children, since children have a minimal amount of cultural conditioning.[6] A study was conducted in which a group of nursery school children of approximately an equal number of males and females was divided into two groups. One group was told a sad story, the other was told a happy story. The children were then given a choice of a brown or yellow crayon to use in coloring the dress on a sketch of a girl. The results showed that those children to whom the happy story was told most frequently chose yellow, while the group to whom the sad story was told most frequently chose the brown crayon. No significant sex differences were exhibited. Thus, it was concluded that nursery school children do have color-mood associations.

Analysis of the spontaneous drawings of kindergarten children followed by interviews suggested that a similar relationship may exist in terms of personal orientation and/or fluctuating moods (as opposed to induced moods).

Much research has been devoted to taking inventory of color preferences under varying conditions of hue, saturation, and brightness. The general conclusions have been that small differences in brightness and saturation do not change the order of preference. Changes in brightness large enough to affect preferences tend to distort the color or to make brightness an overriding feature, which is unrealistic because brightness of this magnitude is rarely encountered in the daily environment and is generally used for special effects. Some investigations have postulated two types of individuals—those who prefer saturated colors and those who prefer unsaturated colors—but the largest part of the evidence indicates that saturated colors are most preferred. Guilford and Smith stated that "colors tend to be liked most at levels of brightness at which they can be most saturated."

Market-research oriented investigators state that color preferences cannot be assessed apart from objects. To the scientific investigator, however, the introduction of products or objects often confounds the issue, as do the elements of time, fashion, and design. Different designs in different years often best lend themselves to different colors. The most popular color for Ford automobiles may be black in the 1940s, cream in the 1950s, and blue in the 1960s. Studies of color preferences per se, however, show that they remain remarkably stable over prolonged periods (one study ran for 14 years) and at a significant level of .01 in many instances. These stability levels are to be expected in phenomena that are assumed to be grounded in personality structure; in fact, they would change only under conditions of prolonged and deep therapy directed toward the restructuring of the personality. Too many books are written on the results of market research. The findings of these surveys often represent little more than fads, so by the time that a book is written and published the results are obsolete and another fad is in vogue.

Although Guilford and Smith worked with the pleasant-unpleasant dimensions of color, it does not appear to be possible to evaluate color on only these two dimensions, and therein lies a weakness with much of the early color research. Recent studies of color have tended to use the Osgood Semantic Differential primarily because of its scaling attributes. It also provides an objective, quantified measure of the connotative meanings of stimuli by the use of bipolar (verbal opposites) adjectives, such as good-bad and beautiful-ugly. The connotative meaning refers to the suggested or symbolic meaning of a stimulus as well as to its explicit meaning.

Although color has been associated with personal characteristics since the world was ruled by the gods, it was not until the publication of the Rorschach Inkblot Method in 1921 in Switzerland that a systematic exploration of the relationship between color preferences and responses and personality traits was begun. Until recent years, most of this research was conducted in Europe. The Color Pyramid Test (CPT), for instance, which is a semistructured, color-oriented, projective instrument, was devised in 1950 by Max Pfister,[7] a Swiss psychologist, and introduced into this country by K. W. Schaie in 1963.[8] Although this device has not been widely used in this country, investigations with it by Schaie and this author have shown it to be a highly effective instrument in discriminating between both normal and abnormal groups. Both of these methods will be discussed in detail later in this chapter.

Luscher has worked commercially and diagnostically with color in Europe for many years. His work was translated, edited, and published as a popular book, *The Luscher Color Test,* in this country in 1965.[9] Most psychologists feel that this type of book, written by a recognized authority, should not have been published for popular consumption. It related various personality characteristics to a person's ranking of several series of colors. Any self-testing material in the area of personality can be dangerous. The layman is given the false impression that he can determine his own personality structure, his weaknesses and strengths in just a few minutes, right in his own home, and this is, of course, incorrect. Decisions made on the basis of this kind of personal diagnosis can lead to unfortunate consequences. Yet, the psychologist can use this kind of instrument along with many others to great advantage in his diagnostic work.

All of these projective devices imply that there is a relationship between a person's color responses and his emotional state or, more basically, his personality traits. Projective inventories avoid the limitation of verbal or written responses in which the subject is required to make a self-appraisal.

One of the most interesting and relevant questions in the type of research on which a good deal of this book is based is whether or not there is a "response bias," a tendency by all subjects to respond in a given direction regardless of the stimulus. Many investigators have considered this phenomenon. I. A. Berg[10] found that when some subjects are not sure of the answers, their responses tend to indicate acquiescence; that is, they choose *true, agree,* or *like* rather than the negative opposites of these terms. Other subjects may lean toward *don't know* or a similarly evasive response.

Another important area of response bias lies in tests where the desirable answer is obvious. To take an extreme example, most people would answer *false* to the question, "Have you ever thought about committing a robbery?" even if at one point in their lives they had such thoughts. Thus it becomes important to structure tests or inventories in such a way that the "right" answers are not obvious.

Because of its affective dimensions and its nonstructured aspects, color would seem to be an ideal experimental device to evoke what might be called untainted answers. M. Sherif and H. Cantril state that "the more unstructured and vague the stimulus field is, the more important are the roles of set and other factors not inherent in the stimulus itself."[11] For my doctoral dissertation, I decided to study the positive and negative responses of people, particularly as related to their status as neurotic, psychotic, or normal.[12] Previous studies had indicated that neurotic-tending persons (defined by M. J. Asch as "a tendency on the part of normal persons to demonstrate behavior on psychological measures of personality similar to that demonstrated by neurotics"[13]) respond negatively more often than normal subjects and that psychotic-tending persons (defined similarly to neurotic-tending) tend to respond affirmatively more often than normal persons. Psychologists have said that the yea-sayers, the psychotic-tending, have given up any kind of battle with their environment, that they are acquiescent in the extreme. Neurotics, on the other hand, are in constant and direct conflict with their environment. Asch used examples from psychoanalytic theory to explain these phenomena. For instance, the obsessive-compulsive neurotic personality is fixated at the anal-retentive stage. In his battle against conformity, he is in conflict with his surroundings so much that his uniform response tends to become negative.

Couch and Kenniston reported clinical interviews that indicated that the mode of ego functioning is what most strongly differentiates the yea-sayers from the nay-sayers.[14] The former have a passive, releasing ego, while the latter have a more active, controlling ego. The receptive egos of the former seem to be an outgrowth of their lack of internalization of parental control in childhood. The nay-sayers, on the other hand, internalize this controlling function in the early years, when they strongly identified with their parents.

C. W. Grant was the first to write a doctoral dissertation on the question of response bias as a personality variable.[15] He used the Minnesota Multi-phasic Personality Inventory as his measure. His results confirmed the hypotheses of neurotic nay-saying and psychotic yea-saying. The neurotic-tending individuals were high on the scale in hypochondriasis, depression, and hysteria. The psychotic-tending individuals were high in hypomania, schizophrenia, psychothenia, and paranoia. I used these same definitions for my color research project, which included 600 people, divided evenly between males and females, between the ages of sixteen and forty-five. The experiment utilized a set of three-by-three-inch deeply saturated colors—red, blue, green, and yellow.

The results supported the hypotheses I was testing: first, the neurotic-tending subjects chose as their favorite colors red and yellow, in that order, and the psychotic-tending subjects chose blue and green, in that order. Thus, the implication is that colors can be used effectively as a personality inventory, perhaps with greater validity than the content factor, since the latter often lends itself to falsification of one kind or another and since the results can be put into practice for color usage where these two groups are concerned.

Edwards developed a personality inventory, the Edwards Personal Preference Schedule,[16] in which he tried to keep measures of social desirability to a minimum because of his contention that self-reports are measures of social desirability—that if the behavior indicated by an inventory item is desirable, the subject will tend to attribute it to himself, and vice versa. Another difference is that the Edwards schedule measures variables that are likely to be attached to the normal individual, whereas a number of the most important personality inventories purport to measure clinical and psychiatric syndromes such as hysteria, mania, and emotional instability.

I administered the Edwards to 600 subjects, 300 males and 300 females, from seventeen to thirty-two. I reevaluated the scales and analyzed the data on an ego-level basis, as follows: Ego+2, Ego+1, Ego-1, Ego-2, with +2 representing greatest strength and -2 representing least strength.

Subjects who preferred red and yellow tended to be in the +2 area on change, autonomy, and dominance; subjects who preferred blue and green scored at the +2 level on endurance. Both groups were at the +1 level on achievement and heterosexuality. Subjects who preferred warm colors scored at the +1 level on exhibitionism, while the cool color group was higher on order. Both groups were about even on affiliation, nurturance, and intraception, and both groups were low on deference and so low on aggression and succor as to make these correlations insignificant.

While the results indicate that warm-color-preferring subjects tend to score somewhat higher on those scales that characterize ego strength, it should also be noted that the cool group also scored high on scales of ego strength of a more orderly, persevering nature.

The unstructured projective method is one of the most widely used techniques in both clinical and personality assessment. The Rorschach Inkblot Method, especially, is often employed in clinical practice.[17] Even with its broad acceptance, it is one of the most often criticized instruments. One of the major criticisms leveled against it is the lack of basal work with "normal" subjects as a criterion against which pathological groups could be compared; otherwise, obtained scores are not always easy to interpret. Another criticism deals primarily with Rorschach's hypothesis that color responses are measures of the affective, or emotional, state. He stated that neurotics are subject to "color shock," as exhibited in a delayed reaction time when presented with a colorblot. He also noted that red evoked the shock response in neurotics more often than did other colors.

Research has not always completely supported his hypothesis, but no method has come along that has proven to be better. The popularity and usage of the Rorschach increase annually, and the weight of the evidence favors the color-affect theory. More specifically, responsiveness to the warm colors (orange, yellow, pink, or red) characterizes emotional impulsivity, and responsiveness to the cool colors (blue or green) characterizes emotional control. Color responses have also been related to a desire for, or feeling against, social participation, ego control, spontaneity versus passivity, and depression. The latter category is the one area of near-unanimous agreement—the diminished interest of the depressed individual in his environment is reflected in his lack of color interest. I believe that more work needs to be done in this area. In some of my investigations several depressed groups have revealed a strong interest in, and preference for, bright, deeply saturated colors. Perhaps color serves as both a stimulant and compensation for lack of emotional tone and color.

The use of the Semantic Differential scales with the Rorschach in recent years has been effective in demonstrating common factors. In previous years most studies tended to be evaluated subjectively. For example, pronounced differences in ratings between achromatic and chromatic cards have been demonstrated consistently. Generally, the chromatic cards have been rated as more positive and pleasant and more active and "good" in terms of factor loadings than the achromatic ones. A comparison between the Rorschach inkblots and the Holtzman inkblots, using a Semantic Differential scale, also showed a pronounced consistency in the rating of the chromatic cards as more positive and pleasant than the achromatic ones.

Physiological measures based on Rorschach responses have given more consistent data than subjective ratings. For example, certain types of color responses have been shown to increase pulse rate, heartbeat, and respiration. In general, the warm colors, especially red, speed things up, and the cool colors, especially neutral shades like gray, make for a slow pace.

Another personality measurement device is the Color Pyramid Test (CPT), which is nonverbal, projective, and minimally structured. In the administration of this personality inventory, the subject is given a five-step pyramid of fifteen fields, one inch square, and colored paper squares. He is then asked to fill in the fields to make first a "pretty" pyramid, then an "ugly" pyramid. The scoring procedures are based on the standardization of the instrument in Germany and later modifications in America. Pyramids can also be classified into those dominated by color, or by form, or an intermediate step between absolute dominance by color or form.

Heiss gives an interpretation of the CPT in terms of high or low color choices.[18] High red is associated with impulsivity, low red is characteristic of reduced emotional tone and responsiveness to stimuli. Orange is an index of extroversion-introversion, with high orange characterizing a highly sociable person, a good mixer, one who is most happy in the company of others. Persons with high yellow scores also have skills in the establishment of interpersonal relations, but they are more objective, cool, and poised in these situations than the emotional high oranges. High black reflects depression, withdrawal, and regression. High purple is characteristic of the emotionally disturbed, anxious individual. Schizophrenic blandness and lack of inhibition control characterize the high white. High browns are negativistic and need-deprived. High blues are introspective and rational in approach, whereas low blues are irrational and poorly organized. High green indicates sensitivity and an active inner emotional life, whereas low greens lack sensitivity and spontaneity and are bland.

K. W. Schaie used the color-form classification of the CPT

to test the hypothesis that if the CPT is a measure of increasing personality differentiation, then a comparison between college students and adolescents should yield significant differences between the two groups.[19] A study of these two groups showed that this was the case and that there was also less variability of choice between color and form in the college group. In other words, the college students rated form over color.

Knapp hypothesized that aesthetic preference as a measure of personality and temperament has many of the same features as the traditional personality inventories.[20] Specifically, aesthetic preference is related to motivation, emotional makeup, the defense mechanisms, and the unconscious. Statistically, there is both variation and consistency between and within individuals. He developed an instrument to measure aesthetic preference and to relate this measure to an established psychological variable called *n* achievement. After an unsatisfactory attempt to develop a test based on the reproduction of paintings, he settled upon a set of pictures of clan tartan figures which he called the Tartan Test. Tartan preference has been correlated with such established measures of personality and interests as the Minnesota Multi-phasic Personality Inventory and the Strong Vocational Interest Inventory. A correlation of the results of tartan preference scores with *n* achievement shows a marked relationship between the color red in tartan preference and low *n* achievement and between the color blue in tartan preference and high *n* achievement.

In an attempt to explain the findings of this test, Knapp postulated that *n* achievement is an ego strategy as well as a need in the classical psychological sense; as an ego strategy, it can be defined as the manner in which one deals with the environment in the pursuit of his goals. Thus, one with high *n* achievement wishes to "do unto" his environment, while one with low *n* achievement wishes to have his environment "do unto" him. (The fact that McClelland[21] was able to measure *n* achievement in preschool children suggests that this feature of personality is autogenetically established in early childhood.) He then made an association between the tartan color preferences, ego strategy, the psychophysics of color and Gestalt psychology. Red, he mused, is inherently brighter than blue, rarely found in nature, and more attention-getting. Consequently, blue is more manipulatable and lends itself to a "ground" frame of reference, whereas red is aggressive, intrusive, and becomes "figure" in the figure-ground phenomenon. (See Chapter 6.) Consequently, those with high *n* achievement prefer blue because they seek a tractable, passive environment they can control and manipulate.

Knapp further hypothesized that the middle class, with their generally high *n* achievement, dress more somberly than do the lower socioeconomic classes, who tend to favor more colorful attire and surroundings and are less achievement-oriented. He uses the example of the "man in the gray flannel suit" as the epitome of subdued middle-class taste. In recent years, the middle class has adopted a more colorful approach to life, and so color preference has become much less important in discriminating between haves and have-nots.

Another approach to the problem of personality measurement through the use of color responses is the eclectic approach. Honkavaara has been one of the most prolific investigators in this area.[22] Her basic hypothesis has been that color-reactors and form-reactors have different orientations and respond to the world in two entirely different ways. She used the Descoeudres' Color-Form Test with a group of college students at Harvard and a group of college students in England and found that, for one thing, form-reactors were more numerous at Harvard. Using descriptions of personality types associated with each of these orientations, she concluded that the color-reactor English students are "highly sensitive, shy, irrational, and individualistic . . . whereas the more practically minded and socially conforming American tends to be a form-reactor." The investigator questioned whether or not America is a more executive-oriented practical nation than a creative-oriented, original one, and whether or not America will become more relaxed and original with time and increasing maturity as a nation.

Using the same overall hypothesis regarding color and form reaction, Honkavaara demonstrated that people who like or prefer persons in a photograph who have been identified as color-reactors have greater perceptual accuracy than those who prefer form-reactors in the photograph or who have no choice.[23] It did not matter whether or not the subjects making the selection from the photograph were themselves color- or form-reactors.

In yet another study, Honkavaara demonstrated a relationship between a person's emotional orientation and his interpersonal preference.[24] Remembering that form-reactors tend to be realistic, socially secure, conforming, and tend to externalize their feelings, whereas color-reactors tend to be irrational, reactive, affectionate, shy, individualistic, and tend to internalize their feelings, she presented two groups of experimental subjects with realistic and poetic pictures. The realistic photos portrayed a Christmas dinner, a mother and child playing, and similar subjects. The poetic photos portrayed a boy looking dreamily out a window, a ballet dancer, and similar subjects.

As hypothesized, like chose like. The investigator concluded that the color-reactors "form a highly talented and creative, but easily destroyed, minority in the American society, and it would be interesting to see how different social classes react to them." A relationship is also indicated between form-reacting and a strong political bent. The implications for choosing a career based on either orientation are worth consideration. It is stated that the selection of an equal number of color- and form-reactors for friends would indicate a realistic emotional attitude, while a preference for color-reactors or ambivalent friends suggests a poetic emotional attitude.

Bjerstadt[25] used a variety of measures, including (1) a task to describe different colors on Semantic Differential scales, (2) a request that subjects construct scenes on variously colored stage floors using ambiguous forms from Twitchell-Allen's Three-Dimensional Personality Test, (3) the administration of prebuilt Color Pyramid technique patterns (which he renamed The Paired Color Pattern Device), and (4) a combination of this latter device with Semantic Differential ratings. The results showed that persons evidencing a preference for warm colors, a predominance of red and yellow patterns, were "stimulus-receptive"; that is, they were active, direct, uncritical in the face of contradictory information, heterosexual, and distractable, that they expressed a need for gratification (life enjoyment), and that they had a short reaction time. Toward the other end of the scale, those preferring cool color patterns (blue and green) were "stimulus selective"; that is, their attention was focused, they critically evaluated information, and they had a high level of concentration. To determine what influence age factor brings to bear on color preference, a study was made of the difference among groups ranging from prep school to university students. The data showed that the younger subjects preferred the warm colors and the older subjects preferred the cool colors.

Another eclectic measure of the excitatory value of colors on a pleasant-unpleasant continuum utilized the GSR (Galvanic-Skin-Response, commonly called the lie detector test) as the criterion instrument. A significant relationship between GSR response and colors that were rated high in excitatory value (reds and yellows) was demonstrated, which explains the emotional factor in this instrument.

It has been generally hypothesized that one of the ways people express their personality is through the clothes they wear. Various studies have tested this theory, and the results have been mixed. An overview of the research suggests that the more secure individual tends to favor colors that range from neutral to cool (green, blue, beige, and gray), of medium value tending toward dull, whereas the more insecure individual tends to select warm, bright colors (red, yellow) that range from the extremes of light and dark.

Crane and Levy studied the relationship between scaling the affective values of color and emotional experience.[26] Colored figures in outline form were presented in each of the following colors: blue, yellow, green, violet, red, and orange. The figures were presented in pairs with questions that had been rated as strong-positive, strong-negative, mild-positive, and mild-negative. Questions that were judged to be pleasant in nature were most frequently associated with red and orange figures and least associated with the violet. The violet figure was most frequently associated with unpleasant questions. The red figure was most frequently associated with the mildly positive, and the blue and green figures with the mildly negative.

My own research has varied widely, and has included both structured and unstructured projective- and content-oriented instruments. In light of this experience, I have concluded that the contradictory results reported by many of the studies are due not only to inadequate sample size and methodology, but also to unrealistic expectations and inadequate experience in personality testing.

There is no reason to assume that a measure of personality has to reach the same level of statistical significance as a physiological or biological response in order to be meaningful. Definitions of personality, intelligence, creativity, and other concepts are such that any instrument constructed on these bases and

69

premises must be interpreted accordingly. The "battery of tests" concept has been instituted because no one test or inventory can be completely trusted to tell the whole story; trends between tests of a similar nature and across tests of a different nature are more reliable indicators of the truth. Dr. Wallace Gobetz, director of the Testing and Advisement Center at New York University, includes an average of twenty-three tests in a battery. Additional tests are included in special cases or in average cases where clarifications are needed. For example, just as an intelligence test score can be interpreted validly only in terms of the subject's exposure to the information requested, so a Rorschach color response can be fully understood only in relation to the patient's behavior, communication, and measures on other protocols. This is equally true for the Minnesota Multiphasic Personality Inventory (a structured instrument). While it is true that research will occasionally show the one-to-one relationship that is so clear and easy to understand (example: delayed reaction time to sudden exposure to the color red indicated a high degree of emotionality), many times this will not be possible because of the subtlety of personality, and the many variables that enter into a testing situation that will generally not be observable in any given situation.

The work of Compton is highly significant in the area of the relationship between a subject's personality and his selection of clothing color and fabric. The Compton Fabric Preference Test[27] utilizes as criterion instruments (measures of personality) the California Psychological Inventory, the Rorschach Inkblot, Kraut Personal Preference Test, Maslow Security-Insecurity Inventory, and the Allport, Vernon, Lindzey Study of Values. Experimental materials include fabrics of large and small design, rough and smooth textures, warm colors (yellow, yellow-orange, orange-yellow, purple) and cool colors (yellow-green, green-yellow, green, blue-purple), saturated colors, shades, and tints.

Using the Compton Fabric Preference Test with one group of delinquent girls and another group of nondelinquent girls, Compton found no significant relationship between body measurement and fabric preferences in the nondelinquent group, but the larger girls in the delinquent group chose warm colors along with weaker contrasts in the figure-ground pattern and smaller designs than did smaller girls.[28]

Compton inventoried the fabric and design preferences of a group of hospitalized psychotic women in terms of the body-image concept as defined by Fisher and Cleveland.[29] Specifically, this study, investigating the relationship between the concepts of body, image boundary (barrier), penetration of boundary, and clothing preference. Boundary of the body can refer to the extension of the self to include parts of the environment: penetration is related to fragility or vulnerability. It is to be expected that persons with mental and emotional problems would be likely to suffer from some aberrated form of body-image. It was found that subjects with weak body boundaries tend to reinforce them with fabrics of strong figure-ground contrasts and brighter, more highly saturated colors. Preference for large designs and warm colors is related to weak penetration scores. Consequently, the role of clothing in providing body-image constancy and invulnerability in new situations for the mentally ill is demonstrated here, and the significance of fashion therapy in mental hospitals and penal institutions is emphasized.

People look at the world in different ways and process the environment in terms of their own dynamics—needs and drives. Two persons looking at the same scene may see it two entirely different ways, one as friendly, the other as hostile. Petrie, McCulloch, and Kadzin[30] studied a normal group and found three perceptual types: **Reducers**—persons who tend to subjectively *reduce* (decrease) perceived size; **Augmenters**—persons who tend to subjectively *increase* perceived size, and **Moderates**—

persons who alter perceived size little or not at all. Other studies have shown that poor children perceive the size of coins as larger than children of greater financial means. Petrie et al.[31] found a significantly greater number of reducers than aug-menters in a group of delinquent boys and girls than in a non-delinquent group. They also noted that this perceptual type had the ability to contain pain and suffering by reducing stimulus intensity. Reducer delinquents, they found, also have a need for bright colors, music, company, change, movement, and speed. In general, delinquents tend to be one of the most inter-esting and productive areas of investigation into the relationship between color preference and personality characteristics in mental illness.

Schizophrenics are generally the most widely tested group of the mentally ill. It is still a point of debate whether this group represents the largest psychiatric division or whether more disturbed people are put into this category for lack of a more accurate diagnosis. At best, schizophrenia seems to be a catchall category for the disturbed young and relatively young.

Perhaps one of the most commonly held theories is that schizophrenics suffer color shock (delayed reaction) upon pre-sentation of the chromatic cards (following the achromatic cards) of the Rorschach inkblots. Slowed reaction time in gen-eral *is*, of course, recognized as one of the behavioral deficits of this group, along with the inability to integrate affective (emotional) experience.

Drawings in a variety of forms have been used to assess psychological functionings—chromatic and achromatic and/or a combination of the two. In a report on color responses to the Thematic Apperception Test (and to projective tests in general and to other free hand or otherwise executed drawings using color), Murstein stated:[32] "The studies, considered as a whole, support the assumption that the addition of color facilitates differentiation between thematic responses of psychiatric and normal, and normal and handicapped groups." In other words, it is assumed that chromatic and achromatic pictures, abstracts, and/or drawings tap different levels of personality, with chromatic material drawing on the emotional aspect. Schizophrenics use black as the predominant color in their drawings significantly more often than do normals. On the abstract-realistic continuum, abnormals in general use individual, personal, and symbolic writing in place of drawing and stereotyped drawings.

A "color stress" factor (C-factor) in response to the Rorschach color plates has been postulated as a discrimination index between schizophrenics and other hospitalized patients. Although the research that has been done on the index as of this writing is generally inadequate, it can be stated that the C-factor in the Rorschach is unquestionably a critical factor in schizophrenic diagnosis when used in conjunction with the results from other instruments.

Schizophrenic adults of severe and mild autism (an escape from reality into either need or wish-fulfilling fantasies) often respond differentially to high- and low-saturated colors. For example, the presentation of high-saturated colors interferes with cognitive functioning for both groups more than does the presentation of low-saturated colors. Interference was greater for patients with severe autism than for those with mild autism, both of whom responded similarly to low-saturated cards. There appears to be a direct relationship between the severity of the illness and the intensity of the response to the degree of saturation.

In color-matching tasks, errors made by normal children are related to the dominant feature of the design; errors made by autistic children are usually of a persevering or alternating nature, thus suggesting an insensitivity to the design and the imposition of stereotyped functioning. The autistic tendency to engage in stereotype and preservation behavior function as a form of security, in that the stress of "set" change is avoided. A deficit or a distortion in the sensory input and processing mechanism is also a factor in autistic functioning.

A study done in Taiwan compared the differences between schizophrenics and normals in a color-usage task.[33] Schizophrenics used fewer colors, were less conventionally oriented, and used more deep green and black than did the normal group. These results are generally in keeping with those obtained in America and suggest that cultural differences are not of great importance in this type of pathology. Schizophrenics frequently suffer from visual problems at the onset and duration of the illness.

A. I. Pevzener studied the course, form, and duration of color-vision disturbances in schizophrenics in therapy.[34] Alterations in color thresholds were also apparent in these patients. The visual problems were accompanied by impaired tactile sensitivity and heightened perceptiveness. Although color vision changed differentially for different colors, the most significant changes were a decrease in sensitivity to red in the acute cases and to blue-green in the chronic cases. Improvement in mental state was reflected in a return to normal color thresholds and a lessening of vision complaints in general.

Various studies have been made of the ratings by psychiatric patients on the effect of lights of different colors on pictures of human faces expressing varying degrees of emotion. Regardless of the emotion expressed, pictures under red light are rated as more active and unpleasant than those under either blue or white light. The influence of color on performance of various tasks suggests an undifferentiated, field-dependent orientation in these groups.

A. Tolor did a study in which he sought to differentiate

between brain-injured patients and psychoneurotics.[35] Using the Color Drawing Test, he found that the psychoneurotics produced a greater number of "blended designs, representations of objects, scenes, people, diagonal, wavy or abstract designs" than did the brain-damaged group. Horizontal or vertical strips or undifferentiated, single-color masses were characteristic of the latter group.

A follow-up study by the same investigator with a new and larger sample produced less definitive results than the first study, but a significant difference was nevertheless maintained.[36] However, Tolor recommends that the Color Drawing Test be used in conjunction with other diagnostic aids; in other words, a battery of tests is much better than just one test.

Perhaps it should be noted that organically affected groups consistently tend to produce drawings that are significantly different from those of other disturbed groups on the Organic Integrity Test, the Color Drawing Test, and on spontaneous drawings.

It has been postulated that form discrimination is the foundation upon which language skills rest; consequently, a measure of color-form dominance in aphasiacs would reflect their reading levels. In turn, the development of form-matching skills would be reflected in an improvement in the reading of this group.

Using color, size, form, number, and orientation match to simple tasks, Wig and Bliss compared the perceptual functioning of a group of adult aphasiacs with that of a group of normal adults.[37] Using Heidbreder's finding that concept performance does not change significantly above the age of eighteen,[38] the researchers made no attempt to equate the groups on the basis of educational level. The stimuli were blue, green, red, and yellow horizontal and vertical hexagons, ovals, rectangles, and triangles in both small and large sizes.

The results for form-matching were almost identical for the two groups; both selected form and size more often than color. However, orientation was preferred to color by the aphasiacs, and color was preferred to orientation by the normals. These findings parallel the overall results on non-brain-damaged adults in that the concrete dimensions of size and form were preferred to the more abstract one of color. It should be noted that this group of aphasiacs exhibited only mild to moderate receptive and expressive dysfunctioning. Other studies have shown poor form-matching and orientation skills among aphasiacs. Perceptual rotations are also common in this group.

As a model for their study described above, Wig and Bliss used Dale's study of the influence of labels on normal children's perception of color.[39] He compared the matching and recognition ability of two groups of children, one that could name colors and another that could not. Both groups performed similarly on the matching dimension, even though some of the children could not overtly name the color. It was assumed that this group used a covert categorizing response. Dale hypothesized that color retention takes two forms: *representational,* relating to physical properties, and *symbolic,* relating to the classification or the naming of the stimulus.

The percentages of subjects who allegedly dream in color have varied quite a bit from investigation to investigation. In a study conducted in the 1950s by Hall, 29 percent of the subjects dreamed in color.[40] Knapp reported 14 percent,[41] Monroe reported 21 percent,[42] and Kahn et al. reported a high of 82.7 percent.[43] In another study of the 1950s, Lovett Doust found that 13 percent of his subjects dreamed in color,[44] while in the 1930s Husband's figure was 40 percent.[45]

The range in percentages here is attributable in large degree to variations in the research methodology used by the different investigators. It has recently been determined that people consistently tend not to voluntarily report color in their dreams unless they are specifically questioned about it. The Kahn figures are related to the fact that they used "careful interrogation close to the time of dreaming," whereas other studies used questionnaires and other techniques that might be considered remote or relatively inflexible. Kahn et al. concluded that:

> The fact that color was present in 70 percent of the dreams, and in 83 percent when the vaguely colored category is included, suggests that dreaming should be considered a colored rather than a black-and-white phenomenon. It would appear that it is the lack of color rather than its presence in dream recall which requires explanation.

Studies of the significance of color in dreams have for the most part been conducted by psychoanalysts. Although Freud regarded color in dreams, as he regarded other sensations, as yet another part of regressive, hallucinatory wish-fulfillment, most investigators now state that inherent physiological processes account for some color in all dreams. Hall concluded that his studies revealed nothing of psychological significance in color dreams:

> We have compared the dreams of people who dream entirely in color with those of people who never dream in color, and have found no difference in any aspect of their dreams. We have compared the colorless dreams of the same person without discovering any way in which they differed. Nor can we find any specific sym-

bolic meaning in a particular color. We are forced to conclude on the basis of our present study that color in dreams is merely an embellishment, signifying nothing in itself.[46]

This investigator did find that 20 percent of over 3,000 dreams had some color in them, and that women reported color in dreams more often than did men, 31 percent to 24 percent. He also found that people over the age of 50 have a slight tendency to have less color in their dreams than those under 50.

Sigmund Freud traced each color in a highly colorful dream to experiences in which each color had originally appeared:

> The scene in which I annihilate P. with a glance forms the center of the dream. His eyes become strange and weirdly blue, and then he dissolves. This scene is an unmistakable imitation of a scene that was actually experienced. I was a demonstrator at the Physiological Institute; I was on duty in the morning, and Brucke learned that on several occasions I had been unpunctual in my attendance at the student's laboratory. One morning, therefore, he arrived at the hour of opening and waited for me. What he said to me was brief and to the point; but it was not what he said that mattered. What overwhelmed me was the terrible gaze of his blue eyes, before which I melted away—as P. does in the dream, for P. has exchanged roles with me much to my relief. Anyone who remembers the eyes of the great master which were wonderfully beautiful even in his old age, and has ever seen him angered, will readily imagine the emotions of the young transgressor on that occasion.[47]

In addition to Freud's conclusion that color in dreams

can be understood as actual reproductions of new and old memory images, he also felt that color in dreams could be symbolic of old sensory impressions or even reflective of the regression that is inherent in the sensory images of a dream. P. Greenacre has suggested that the shock reaction from seeing the paternal phallus may be represented by the color in a dream.[48]

Calef[49] and Knapp[50] associate color in dreams with the emergence of voyeuristic-exhibitionistic impulses and conflicts. Yazmajian, using case histories, explains this theory in terms of ego functions that disguise representation of "childhood memory traces of the color contrasts perceived on viewing genitals and pubic hair of adults and children."[51] An example of this might be a dream of a red table that in reality would be symbolic of red pubic hair observed as a child.

One of the most thorough and practical studies in this area was conducted by Suinn, who sought to determine personality type based on Jung's typology and color dreaming.[52] Personality type of the experimental subjects was determined by the use of the Myer-Briggs Indicator, which is a personality inventory based on the Jungian theory of personality types, extroversion-introversion, sensation-intuition, thinking-feeling, and judgment-perception. Personality scores were then correlated with the frequency of color dreams, proportion of color dreams as compared with all dreams, vividness of color in dreams, and pervasiveness.

The results indicated that there are two kinds of color in dreams, reality color and symbolic color: the former is a reflection of the conscious world; the latter is symbolic of inner processes. The individual who responds objectively and in detail to his environment has dreams that are often a duplication of his daytime environment. The individual who reacts to experience with emotion and in a highly personalized way tends to dream in symbolic color; color in dreams represents for him emotions as part of his makeup or the failure to discharge or clarify an emotional situation or experience. Suinn also found a significant relationship between introversion and frequency of color for males.

Vividness of color dreams characterized the reality-oriented type in males and the emotional female; thus, these polar opposites reflected further sex differences in the handling of dream content.

Women characterized as emotional had a greater frequency and proportion of color dreams than did the other types. The investigation's overall conclusion is that "men tend to duplicate the objective characteristics of their reality environment when they dream . . . [women] appear to respond more to the unconscious determinants of dream content." Further analysis of this study indicates that the extroverted, reality-oriented male has a higher proportion of color dreams, a greater degree of vividness and pervasiveness than does the introverted, thinking type of male. Women of an extroverted orientation have a greater frequency and proportion of color dreams than do other personality types. However, women of the "intuition" type have greater vividness in the color of their dreams.

Husband attributes the fact that women tend to dream in color significantly more often than do men to their vivid and imaginative natures.[53] Middleton found that women reported the colors of clothing in their dreams, but men rarely report these.[54] The only color image reported that was common to both sexes was red fire. Blank, a psychoanalyst who has worked with blind patients, reports that the congenitally blind, along with most of those blinded before the age of five, do not have visual dreams.[55] However, those who are blinded after the age of seven tend to retain visual memory and visual dream imagery. Instead of visual elements in their dreams, the congenitally blind imagine such nonvisual elements as speech, smell, and other sensory elements.

5/The perception of color

While the material in this book has been drawn primarily from the area of psychology and design, there is another discipline that, while highly technical and specialized, does have some relevance to the subject under discussion. This is the physical aspect of color—its perception by the viewer, its composition, and so on. A tremendous amount of research has been done in this large area, mostly by physical scientists. In this chapter we will attempt to cover the most pertinent aspects of their work, especially in the twentieth century.

Some investigators have demonstrated a difference in the spatial expressions of saturated hues with a long wavelength, specifically the so-called warm colors, red, orange, and yellow. Gerda Smets postulated a difference in time expression.[1] Specifically, the time interval spent before a warm color is perceived as shorter than that spent before a cool color. Fifty-four subjects were randomly presented with a red filter and a blue filter under the conditions of first giving no indication of what would be asked of them regarding the stimuli. A second group of seventy-five subjects was presented with the same stimuli with the instructions to say "stop" when the second stimulus was seen as long as the first one. The perceived time interval before red was shorter than that for green. The investigator also noted that a strong order effect was evident; that is, although the exposure time for both colors was objectively equal, the perceived time interval was shorter for the first exposed color. Some more recent studies have shown that brightness rather than hue is the critical feature in the perception of a color as near or far.

Wilson's finding that the arousal value of red is superior to that of green is undoubtedly related to the fact that the perceived time interval spent before exposure to the color red is perceived as shorter than that spent before the exposure to green.[2] Wilson used the conductance level of the Galvanic Skin Response (GSR) (lie detector test) as a measure of arousal value. Again, the order of presentation of stimuli was such a feature that the measure of conductance level tended to be obscured; however, in the measure of rapid conductance changes there was a difference in favor of red. This finding supported the subjects' subjective reports that variously indicated that red was the "more stimulating, exciting, awakening, attention-getting, overpowering and lively."

Another area of interest is the feedback-conditioning phenomenon. B. B. Brown, one of the most active investigators in the field, stated that "It is apparent that when individuals can perceive information about their own physiology, they can experience interacting with specific components of their physiology and then develop voluntary control over these functions."[3] He conducted a study in which experimental subjects were requested to attempt identification of mood and feeling states that would keep on a blue light operated solely by Electroencephalogram (EEG) alpha activity. Specifically, the subjects were told that brain activity reflected thinking and feeling states and that the brain activity, as recorded, could be converted into a force that could turn on a blue light. Written EEG records reflected frequency and amplitude values of alpha activity.

No external stimuli were used, but rather a closed physiological feedback system to the circuit was employed; that is, the subjects were requested to identify nonverbally a feeling state that could keep the light on. Practice sessions ranged from one to four in frequency for different subjects. Their eyes were open during both the experimental and the rest periods. EEG activity was recorded bipolarly from the temporaparietal and occipital sites of the right hemisphere. The subjects were also requested to signal by a light switch in the recording room when they recognized the selected feeling state with which to operate the blue light. The level of enhanced alpha activity appeared to be related to those subjects "who lost awareness of all environmental factors except the light, or who felt dissolved in the environment," and to pleasing feeling states in general.

The abundance of alpha activity when related to type of evaluation of time varied widely; "however, the majority of higher levels of discrimination were paired with reports of either no awareness of time of the session or to the feeling that the elapsed time was short."

Brown had previously experimented with external stimuli (colored lights) as the triggering device for EEG activity.[4] The percentage content of alpha, beta, and theta activity in the EEGs of each of 45 subjects was recorded. The intensity of the three colored lights was then scaled to the amplitude of its EEG wave. Frequency range and colored lights were then randomly paired. After several practice sessions, the experimental subjects were requested to sort 105 descriptors of mood and feeling to match their feelings when each of the three colored lights was activated by their own alpha, beta, and theta activity. An analysis of the results indicated at least two kinds of descriptors—"those specific to EEG frequency independent of color (e.g., calm to alpha, afraid to beta), and those predominantly associated with color (e.g., excited to red, sad to blue)." It should also be noted that a control group of 45 subjects sorted the same descriptors as to red, blue, and green. The descriptors could be sorted to a no-color category by both the experimental and the control group.

Dr. Manfred Clynes and Michael Kolin of the Rockland State Hospital in Orangeburg, New York, found that "each different color elicited a characteristic pattern in the brain's electrical activity," as recorded by a computer.[5] Dr. Clynes found that although there are variations in color patterns across many recordings, a characteristic pattern emerges for each color. He also found such pattern change according to the placement on the scale of the two recording electrodes. "For example, two electrodes placed one above the other on the back of the head will record one pattern for a particular color, whereas a side by side horizontal arrangement of the electrodes will produce another pattern with the same color stimulus."

These findings give further evidence of the localizations of the brain processes and, in turn, may ultimately result in a fixed mapping of the brain. It is suggested that this research should enable scientists to differentiate between colorblindness that results from a defect in the retina of the eye and that caused by a nerve or brain defect.

One of the most widely known and quoted studies on the effect of color surroundings is that by K. Goldstein, in which he found that a limited number of brain-damaged cases responded "expansively" to red and "contractively" to green.[6] Further, he found his patients responded in an excited manner to red and in a calm manner to green. When his patients were asked to place their arms in given positions, move them at a given rate of speed, or to estimate time, size, length, weight, and cutaneous localization, he found a greater outward movement of the arms at a greater rate of speed under red than under green. Under red conditions, subjects who had already shown a preexisting tendency either to overestimate or to underestimate the time intervals, due to brain damage, showed a continued or exaggerated tendency toward inaccuracy, whereas all subjects tended to judge more accurately under green. Psychophysical judgments of size, length, weight, and touch were found to be less accurate under red than under green.

Goldstein's findings and theories have been widely attacked and investigated because of the fact that his subjects were brain-damaged, and it was felt that the results could not be extrapolated to normal subjects; also, his sample size was quite small (from two to five subjects), and his study lacked a sufficient degree of methodological rigor. Nevertheless, his overall findings, if not always the specifics, have withstood the challenges to which they have been subjected.

Using different colored lights, Gerard found that red had a more rousing effect on the functions of the autonomic nervous system and on visual cortical activity than did blue.[7] He also found that red evoked more tension, excitement, and hostility than did blue. J. S. Nakshian duplicated Goldstein's study with a group of normal subjects and found that there was significantly greater hand tremor under red than under green, and on the motor inhibition task, where speed of movement is the key factor, the performance was significantly faster under red than under green.[8] However, measures of accuracy of judgments of length, reproduction of time intervals, and arm movements did not responsibly support the Goldstein findings. Perhaps it should be noted that the two tasks in which the two colors were found to have opposite effects share a common factor of measuring inhibitory control over motor expression. The investigator concluded that his findings might be explained in terms of Goldstein's theoretical concepts: because red induces motor excitation, it would tend to interfere with control of motor activity; because green induces motor relaxation, there is no thrust toward motor activity, and thus motor control tends to be easier.

Halpern and Kugelmass gave reaction-time tests by placing filters of different colors over the eyes of subjects who had the sensorimotor induction syndrome in unilateral disequilibrium due to brain damage.[9] The results showed that reaction times obtained with the red filter were longer and/or more variable than those obtained with the green filter; yellow produced intermediate results; there was a general aggravation of the sensory and motor functions under red, which was corrected under green.

A study by James and Domingos investigated the color environment by lighting one room with a red light and lighting another room with a white light as a control.[10] The results showed a greater degree of hand tremor under the red light than under the white light. Tests at Yale University indicated that bright colors dull the wits.[11] Mental activity at all levels—problem solving, decision making, or social conversation—was affected. Red was found to be the biggest villain, green was next. The more these colors predominated in a room, the greater was the emotional stimulation and presumably the greater interference with reason and memory. (An acquaintance of mine read this information after she had begun planning the color scheme for a college library. She recommended a blue and red combination, after some study and experimentation, on the basis that many students need the serenity of blue while studying, but many others need the stimulation of red to stay awake.)

When Albers characterized color as the most relative of phenomena, he was referring primarily to the fact that perceived color is reflected color, and thereby may have variations in shade, tone, and depth. Color memory fluctuates, too, so that individuals initially perceive colors differently; some see a red as a pure red, while others see hints of yellow or blue in the same red. Even though these physiological differences in color perception by people with normal vision have long been studied and written about, it is still popularly assumed that persons with normal color vision see colors similarly.

Color-normals are generally divided into two groups which are characterized by a bimodal distribution. Rubin, using a monochromator adjusted by his experimental subjects to what they said was the purest green, found that, for a majority of his color-normal subjects, the spectrum locus for pure green was 514 NM; it was 525 NM for a minority of the subjects.[12] Pure green was defined as a shade that has neither a yellow nor a blue cast. The spectrum locus at 525 NM (in the long wave portion of the distribution) is labeled "unique green" and is said to represent a balance between the blue and yellow sensations. Richards also studied the "unique green" phenomenon.[13] He labeled the two different types of normals as group I and group II, based, respectively, on the shorter and the longer spectrum locus of pure spectrum green.

Studying the deuteranomals, a group in which abnormally large proportions of green are necessary to make spectrum matches, and the protanomals, in which similar proportions of red are required for a spectrum match, Rubin found that 583 NM was the locus for the latter; 520 and 502 NM were loci for pure green; and 612 and 590 NM were loci for balanced orange.

Using the anomaloscope, Waaler found a similar bimodality for blue.[14] His two groups of male subjects with normal vision had "blue points" at 487 and 479 NM. Scanning from the blue-green side, the subject indicated the point at which the green dropped out and, from the opposite side, the point at which lilac or dark blue dropped out and a pure blue remained.

Describing the subjects at these two spectrum loci, he stated that, "There is a very clear difference in the individual perception of colour at these two points." He also found similar female blue points with an intermediate group at 483 NM. Further, he postulated a genetic basis for this phenomenon.

The normal eye discriminates three pairs of color—light-dark, yellow-blue, and red-green. The person who sees all three of these pairs is called a trichromat. A person who has lost one of these systems but has the use of two others is referred to as a dichromat. A person who has lost both chromatic systems, with only the light-dark dimension remaining, is referred to as a monochromat. Red-green blindness is the most common form of this abnormality, and blue-yellow blindness, in which red-green discrimination remains intact, is the rarest. Total colorblindness (with light-dark discrimination intact) falls somewhere in between red-green and blue-yellow blindness in incidence. The red-green blind see blues and yellow in much the same manner as does the color-normal, but these colors are seen in combination with gray instead of with the reds and green that may be in evidence. Examples of his color vocabulary are the designation "green" for a low-saturation grayish yellow and "red" for similarly perceived fire engine.

Color deficiencies are much more prevalent among men than among women. Approximately 7 percent of the male population is affected by either color weakness or colorblindness, but less than 1 percent of the female population is similarly affected.

The three major theories of color vision include the Young-Helmholtz theory, which postulates three kinds of cones or cone substances to account for red, green, and blue. A second theory, by Hering, emphasizes the color pairs of black-white, red-green, and blue-yellow. He postulates a building-up and a breaking-down process in which one member of a color pair was yielded in the process. The phenomena of contrast and after-image were used as examples of the process; the fact that the afterimage is in a contrasting color proves the reverse process.

The Ladd-Franklin theory utilized colorblindness as the foundation for an evolutionary process in which light-dark vision represented the most primitive form, blue-yellow more advanced, and finally red-green the most advanced.

One of the more recent theories of colorblindness is that as men have changed from a hunting and gathering society to an agricultural way of life and finally to an industrial society, there has been a relaxation of selection pressures. This theory is in keeping with Katz's "biological color,"[15] in which an animal's survival (and man's, at an earlier period) depends on keen color vision. The more primitive the people, the more they depend on color as a means of identifying essential features in the environment.

One might postulate that projected decline of vegetation and animal life as a result of environmental pollution will produce a monochromatic universe and a return to the primitive light-dark visual system from which man evolved.

A great many studies have been made on the various facets of colorblindness, particularly as it relates to the perception of everyday items and can be compared with normal vision. In the field of mental disorders, for instance, Grunewald and Hapten found that of twelve psychiatric patients categorized as colorblind, only eight were so classified when tested with Nayel's anomaloscope.[16] Perseverance on an incorrect number or the failure to respond within the 15-second time limit were given as the two major areas of failure. Tracing the number in question with the finger facilitated the correct response. The authors concluded that psychiatric problems can lead to the misclassification of some colorblind patients; consequently, these factors should be considered in the testing of psychiatric groups.

White and Price found that older males who scored in the organic range on tests of cortical deterioration also tend to be classified as red-green deficient on the basis of pseudo-isochromatic tests.[17] However, further testing on the Spiral Aftereffects and the Memory-for-Designs as well as the Dworine tests indicates that the poor performance of the perceptually impaired group is attributable to figure-ground confusion rather than defective color vision.

Gilbert's study essentially supports that of Chapanis in stating that there is a steady decline in color discrimination that is related to age, especially in the blue and green areas.[18] This has been attributed to the yellowing of the lens with advancing years. Studies have consistently shown a significant increase in the accuracy of color discrimination between the ages of two and six, but it is not until after about the fifteenth year that children can discriminate colors as accurately as adults can.

Although Gilbert found variability in color aptitude in all age categories, no statistically reliable set differences in variability were found between the sexes below the ages of seventy and eighty. Above this age range, men were found to be more variable than women. However, the total female group (all ages) is superior to the total male group (all ages) in differentiating shades of red and shades of green. The females also obtained higher total color scores in the 10- to 20-year-old group, the 40 to 50 group, and the 70 to 80 group. The investigator hypothesized that the female superiority in the red-green area of the spectrum is possibly attributable to the greater incidence of undetected red-green weakness in the male population.

Wide individual differences in color matching were found in the sixties. All color matching—except yellow, which peaks in the forties—shows an increase from ages ten to nineteen, a peak in the twenties, and a steady decline thereafter. Red and yellow color matching is superior to other colors at all age levels.

The implication for colorists in the industrial area is that women may have a slight advantage over men in this occupational category. Periodic testing and the initial hiring of persons with exceptionally fine ability in color discrimination might be useful procedures in industry.

The incidence of colorblindness among males and females

of various racial and cultural groups is described in the accompanying table.

Prevalence of Colorblindness Among Different Races

Race	Percentage of Colorblindness	
	Men	Women
North American Caucasian	8.0	1.0
German	8.0	0.4
Chinese	6.5	1.7
Turk	5.3	0.0
North American Negro	3.8	0.0
Mexican	2.3	0.6
North American Indian	2.0	0.0

*From L.A. Faas (Ph.D. dissertation, Utah State University, 1966).

A supervisor of occupational therapy at the Industrial Home for the Blind, Institute of Rehabilitation, Jamaica, New York, J. C. Wheeler presents a series of ideas for both teachers of the blind and their pupils in the understanding of color for the blind pupil.[19] The first step in the color teaching procedure should utilize concepts that are either demonstrable to the blind person or already in his frame of reference. At this point, the teacher should stress the concepts of association, incorporation, and retention and the color dimensions of hue, saturation, and brightness. The student is then introduced to each color. For example, yellow is the color of sunlight, gaiety, laughter, and energy. Its eye-catching quality is mentioned, and finally association is made between yellow and such foods as bananas.

Red is the color of love, passion, and anger; it is hot, vivid, and restless. Mention is made of its use in the American flag, as a "stop" traffic signal, and in valentines.

Blue is represented as the color of dignity, poise, and reserve. It is associated with the U.S. flag, the policeman's and sailor's uniforms, and the decor of restful rooms.

Green is described as combination of the "gaiety of yellow and the dignity of blue, and also the predominant color in nature, and is the color of the forest and the jungle. Because of its restful nature it is frequently used in decorating."

Purple is represented as a color of dignity, majesty, wealth, and splendor. It is associated with the reverence and somberness of a funeral and, in its lighter shades, with gay decorating.

Earth colors are cited as examples of brown—it is a rich, dark, healthy, and vital outdoor color. Its neutrality in wood lends itself to any decorating color scheme. It is an autumn color and a popular color for clothing.

Black is described as the color of night, mysterious and somber on the one hand, rich and dignified on the other. Although black is traditionally associated with mourning and loss in the Western world, it offers a striking and dramatic contrast to other colors in clothing and furnishings.

Gray is represented as a conservative color, quiet and calm, it is a reflective color that takes on some of the characteristics of adjacently placed colors. Gray hair and the gray flannel suit are described as dignified. Its neutral quality makes it an excellent background color.

White is most commonly associated with purity, innocence, holiness, and cleanliness. White is the color of the uniforms of doctors, nurses, and most persons handling food. White, especially in recent years, has become one of the most widely used colors in decorating.

The following is a summary of the "personalities" of the colors written for use with children.[21] It has been used with some success, in conjunction with other teaching techniques, to develop some feeling for color and some motivation for studying the subject. To implement the verbal descriptions, one might compare each color to certain types of texture, sound, or physical motion. With young children, this technique enables them to form more concrete associations to the "affect" of a color. One must be careful, however, to avoid fostering misconceptions such as the following: "If red is like the sound of a blaring trumpet, then all trumpets are red."

> Red says: I am bright, hot, and loud. I'm used for stop signs and stop lights, because people can see me from a long way off. Wear me when you feel full of energy, because I like to move around and make noise. When I am mixed with white, I turn into pink, and that calms me down and makes the girls like me. They use me for lipstick and nail polish, but everyone knows me in tomatoes, strawberries and fire engines.
>
> Orange says: I, too, am bright, active and noisy, but not as common as red. People get tired of me very easily, and only use me in small quantities. I have a lot of fun, especially at Halloween, because I like to get into mischief. I'm sometimes hard to get along with, and I like a good fight with purple and red, so don't put us together. You'll find my tangy flavor in oranges and tangerines.[20]

Not all color perception has to do with the sense of seeing through the eyes. The term synesthesia, which can be defined as the subjective image of a sense other than the one being stimulated, can be applied to the ancient art of "finger vision." This phenomenon seems to have been more common in the Soviet Union than in other areas.

In 1962, a 22-year-old epileptic patient, Rosa Kuleshova, was discovered to be able to read print by moving her fingertips over the lines. According to *Time* magazine, Rosa could distinguish between black and white with her toes, and she read the business card of a *Life* correspondent with her elbow.[21] Her experimenters said that Rosa was able to see when the heat rays, but not the light rays, were blocked. Biophysicist Mikhail Smirnov exclaimed, "The fingers have a retina."

One of the most active adherents and investigators of dermo-optical perception (DOP) in the United States has been R. P. Youtz.[22] He has worked with Barnard College students in groups and with one female subject in particular. His initial testing with the experienced female subject yielded highly significant results for color discrimination, especially red and blue. Later testing under tighter controls yielded results at the chance level, but he attributed these failures to cold weather (which would affect heat emission) and to fatigue (and presumably a lowered level of sensitivity to temperature changes). The Barnard students were less skillful than his experienced female subject. He tentatively asserts, however, that DOP ability exists in an elementary form in 10 percent of his female college student samples. The statistical analysis of the results of his tests yielded a low significance level (.001). A further analysis of his data indicates that appropriate consideration was not given to the possible influence of learning curves as well as the effect of up to 600 judgments on a predicted standard error. Perhaps it should be noted that Youtz, in contrast to Soviet scientists, attributes the DOP phenomenon to the ability to sense and to discriminate between delicate temperature changes.

The theory of dermo-optical perception is generally based on a knowledge of infrared radiant energy. Sir William Herschel, the English astronomer, discovered in 1800 that the sun's spectrum contained electromagnetic energy of longer wavelength than red light. But it was not until 1840 that E. W. Herschel, the son of the discoverer and himself a pioneer in the field of photography, recorded these invisible wavelengths on paper, thus forming what he named a thermogram based on infrared radiation. Thermograms are not based on the conventional infrared technique of photography, which uses a filter to remove visible light from the camera, leaving it sensitized to radiation of slightly longer wavelengths than red light. Thermograms are photographic reproductions of infrared radiations which every object whose temperature is above that of absolute zero emits.

According to Barnes, the "human skin is an almost perfect emitter of infrared radiation in the spectral region beyond 3 microns."[23] Consequently, one of the theories of "finger vision" is based on the differential rate of absorption of infrared radiation emitted by the different colors by different layers of the skin. The absorption of radiant energy, from the visible or the nonvisible areas of the spectrum, inevitably results in a rise in the temperature of the absorbing entity (in this case the fingertips) with identification based on the depth of absorption (penetration) of the various wavelengths.

Using a box that supposedly eliminated all sources of illumination as well as any chance of peeking, Youtz tested subjects on color identification. The energy source for identification of the objects was the human skin, which radiated energy that was absorbed by the test objects and then emitted at their own respective wavelengths. These rays penetrate the skin at different depths and heat occurs at the depth at which the rays are absorbed, so the subject identifies the object or color on the basis of either differences in temperature or differences in depths of penetration.

Youtz used the study by Hardy and Muschenheim[24] to show that penetrating infrared has a wavelength of 1.2 microns and a skin penetration of at least 3.0 microns for both the infrared and the visible wavelengths. Oppel and Hardy[25] demonstrated the possibility of quantifying dermal light sensitivity by using nonpenetrating infrared radiation of 0.4 - 0.7 microns and penetrating infrared of 0.8 - 3.0 microns, with an exposure time of three seconds, over a 14.5 cm. area of a human forehead; the subjects responded with "on" when they detected the stimulus. The obtained ratios, using the method of limits, were 2.2:1.5: 1.0 for the evocation of an "on" response for visible wavelengths over penetrating infrared and nonpenetrating infrared radiation.

Buckhout did a study of dermal color discrimination using three-inch squares of red, orange, yellow, green, blue, purple, brown, gray, black, and white which were mounted on black paper under a plastic film.[26] Two identical and one odd color square were mounted on a plate. The subjects placed their hands through two armholes into a blackened cardboard box, where they were to identify the odd color by feel. His results were similar to those of Youtz in that he did have some high-scoring subjects who, on retesting, had a significant performance. But Buckhout, unlike Youtz, neither accepts these findings as proof that some people actually do have dermal light sensitivity nor completely denies its existence. Stating that influence of a good performance based on chance alone would unrealistically elevate overall performance, he questions a research design and statistical analysis that adds trials and observations together. Beyond this, the standard error decreases as the number of observations increase, thus decreasing the established chance level. In other words, few subjects out of a large group will generally have high scores based on chance alone. A high degree of replicability by the high scorers would be essential to lend support to the existence of the phenomenon in question. Consequently, he recommends a more rigorous, preestablished statistical criterion in further study of dermal light sensitivity.

Makous concedes the possibility of identifying the color of objects under study.[27] Red objects, he states, would have low spectral emissivities in the longer wavelengths of the visible spectrum, and blue objects high emissivities in the wavelengths. Consequently, due to the adjacent position of red and infrared,

red would be more likely to have low emissivities than blue. Yellow would emit according to its intermediate spectral position. Using the transmission rate of colored glasses (Hodgman et al.[28]) as a reference source, a researcher could possibly obtain statistically reliable measures of differences in skin temperature in terms of hue, especially at each end of the visual spectrum.

Makous' correlation of .574 (P .05) between the subject's hand temperature differential and the surroundings with her performance lends credence to his hypothesis, which has been referred to as cutaneous emissive sensitivity.

One of the most thorough and recent studies of "finger sight" was conducted by Zavala et al.[29] They tested a subject who had demonstrated cutaneous sensitivity. This subject's performance on the discrimination of colors of plastic discs, projected lights, and playing cards was compared with that of three controls (subjects with no demonstrated sensory ability in that area) and with that of chance. Precautions were taken in the form of a mask, tape, and a bib-screen box to eliminate all possible visual cues. In view of the accusations of peeking leveled against the persons reported to have finger vision, a professional magician was engaged to make certain that no sleight-of-hand or peeking took place.

The stimuli in the poker chip experiment included discriminations between red and blue, blue and white, and red and white. The results showed that, overall, the experienced subject did significantly better than the control group; however, individuals within the group performed above chance in several instances. For example, two of the control subjects performed significantly better than the experienced subject on the red-white discrimination.

Using only the colors red and blue, one variation on the poker chip experiment included discriminating between mounted chips and playing cards. The control subject who compared favorably with the experienced subject in sensitivity to red in the poker chip experiment also showed the same pattern of discrimination between red and blue, but to a lesser extent, as did the experienced subject, who performed significantly better than the control group did.

Another study in this series involved making form discriminations by naming the cards in a deck. Responses were scored only if both the suit and the number were correctly named. The experienced subject performed significantly better than chance and better than the controls, who did not perform better than chance.

The investigators concluded that, given the differences that exist among people, it may be reasonable to assume that there may be differences in distribution of receptors (nerve endings) in various parts of the body including the fingers, along with differences in depth or surface nearness in different individuals, that would account for the sensitivity to stimuli. Mention is also made of the possibility that in the biological evolutionary process there may be a residue of sensitivity to energy.

Although studies of "finger vision" have been handicapped by many persons who have been something less than honest in their ability to discriminate by the "sense of feel," a sensational press, and a skeptical public, it should not be forgotten that the scientists who have studied this phenomenon have sought to determine whether or not there are additional sensory structures, or a different arrangement of nerve endings than previously determined as an aid to enlarging the perceptual world of the blind.

Although the reported incidences of color "hearing," "taste," and "smell" vary among investigators—Diserens[30] reported that 30 percent of the children studied reported color hearing, and Mudge[31] reported that 42 out of 50 reported color or brightness associated with certain tones, musical keys, and instruments—there is little doubt that the phenomenon of cross-modality or synesthesia does exist. Psychedelic drugs have been successful in eliciting responses across sensory mechanisms. LSD has been reported to translate sensory experiences across modalities. For example, observed colors have been felt to beat to music, and vibrations of music have been felt inside of the listener's body.

Diserens discussed the colored hearing phenomenon thus: "Colored hearing is a condition in which sounds (vowels or musical tones) produce a simultaneous sensation of a definite color. For example, in nine cases studied by Claparede, colors were attributed to all or almost all the notes of the scale. A number of persons ascribed colors to musical intervals and represented sharps or flats by slight changes in tint. Entire musical selections or the work of particular composers may induce particular colors, which may also vary with the mood of the music, or the type of instruments played upon."

Singer found that subjects who experienced prolonged and regular color hearing would possibly find it an adverse factor in the pursuit of a musical career.[32] Downey reported a study in which a subject reported color taste, for example, a strong essence of wintergreen evoked pink, cinnamon candy evoked brown, pepper evoked orange-red, a lime water evoked a golden color, strong solutions of sugar and weak solutions of saccharin as well as anise, cherry syrup, and sarsaparilla syrup evoked the color black.[33]

First the subjects' nostrils were plugged; then the subjects' nostrils were unplugged, and the colors became more persistent and intensive. The author was tempted to conclude that the olfactory sense played a major role in color taste until it was recalled that odorless taste stimuli aroused color responses; consequently, it was concluded that while taste and odor modalities intensify color sensations, each is a distinct phenomenon.

D. T. Sharpe, using 100 subjects between the ages of 18-35, with instructions to associate the scent of the five perfumes used in the experiment with the colors red, yellow, blue, green, and purple, found that the subjects agreed in the differentiation of the scent-color categories slightly better than chance.[34]

Synesthesia is an area of study that has unlimited possibilities for the future. It may be that not only will the blind be able to "see" and experience fully the pleasure of colors, but also that this is a mode of communication that will become more and more important to normal people. Further experimentation, and discrimination between charlatans and subjects who genuinely have this ability, must be made before we can ascertain anything more concrete about this most interesting phenomenon.

6/Gestalt and color

With the recent significant increase of concept borrowing across the fields of science and art, it seems only natural that the principles of Gestalt psychology—with its emphasis on figure-ground organization, configuration, and patterning—could be extrapolated to the field of color and design. This does not seem far-fetched, especially when compared to the impact that the methodology of the "field" concept of physics—as begun by Faraday, Maxwell, and Hertz in the nineteenth century—had on electromagnetic fields, a development that culminated in Einstein's theory of relativity and was ultimately also used by Kurt Lewin as the foundation on which to expand Gestalt psychology into a broader concept.[1]

Gestalt psychology was developed in Germany around 1912 by Wertheimer,[2] Koffa, and Kohler and is concerned primarily with the organization of mental processes: experiences depend on the patterns that stimuli form and on the organization of experiences. The figure-ground phenomenon is one of its major principles. In other words, our responses at any given time depend on our mental organization at that time; things or events are responded to as figure or ground (important or less important, respectively). Similarity, continuity, and closure also affect our responses.

"Field" is used in physics to describe a magnetic area encompassing patterns of lines of attraction and repulsion. Lewin used "field" to describe an organization of psychological events—the psychological environment. For purposes of color and design, "field" can be used to describe the living, working. or playing space—the house, office building, school, and so on. It can be anything from a one-room flat to a skyscraper. In fact, in the area of design, *field* is a more dynamic, idea-provoking, action-packed concept with which to work than such designations as space, room, or hall. The vocabulary of design can become more flexible and energized, for example, the living room as a living "field" somehow becomes less furniture-packed, more mobile and flexible. The dining "field" becomes two small tables and chairs rather than the traditional large set of table and chairs.

In my own design work, I have found that designating the features that are to represent figure and those that are to represent ground as a first step on the job eliminates the trial and error inherent in the beginning stages of most creative tasks.

The figure-ground phenomenon is an outgrowth of man's need to impose order and meaning on his environment. It is both a concrete and an abstract phenomenon—concrete as the physical world is observed, abstract as the psychological world is perceived. In the abstract psychological sense, those things of significance at any given moment are determined by the dominance of a person's needs, drives, motives, and experience in his hierarchical system at a given time. This accounts for the fact that the same environment is often perceived in two entirely different ways by two individuals: one person might see a situation as threatening, another might see it as harmonious.

On the other hand, a concrete figure-ground configuration is more stable in its perception, even though some individuals will see figure where most individuals see ground and vice versa. In either case, because of man's need to organize his environment into these two elements for his own sense of stability and meaning, it follows that a setting with organization along the lines of figure-ground will have a pleasing aspect.

Although there are few hard-and-fast rules regarding the achievement of figure-ground organization, color and pattern are the most commonly used methods. E. R. Hilgard, the internationally known psychologist, author, and professor at Stanford University, describes the figure-ground phenomenon in the following manner:

> Geometric patterns are always seen against a background and thus appear object-like, with contours and boundaries . . . .Patterns do not have to contain identifiable objects to be structured as figure and ground. Patterns of black and white and many wallpaper designs are perceived as figure-ground relationships, and very often figure and ground are reversible. Note that the part seen as figure [see the next page] tends to appear as slightly in front of the background, even though you know it is printed on the surface [of the] page. You seem to look through the spaces in and around the figure to a uniform background behind, whether the background is in white (or a light color) or black (or a dark color).[3]

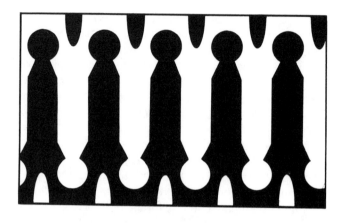

Generally, in interior design, patterned furniture coverings and/or brightly covered furniture against a medium to neutral floor and walls give the room a furniture-figure conformation. In a designed room, dark walls and floors traditionally were treated as ground regardless of furniture treatment, but this is no longer necessarily true—dark floors and walls can emerge as figure against furniture of medium shades and, in some cases, fine prints. Walls that are used for the display of paintings, objets d'art, elaborate wall coverings, and/or window treatments emerge as figure, and in order to keep a unified flow of figure, the floors should be in the same or similar hue, lest the figure-ground relationship becomes fragmented. As a general rule, furniture is one unit of the figure-ground organization, and the walls and the floor are another unit. If light-colored floor covering is to be used with light-colored furniture, a good figure-ground relationship is retained proportionately better if the floor covering is limited to the general space covered by the furniture rather than the total floor area.

The current tendency to fuse figure-ground with patterns

on walls, floors, and furniture gives a soothing, womblike, cocoon feeling of unified action to some, but to others it is too fragmented, hence unsettling and anxiety-provoking. Although this style of decorating seems to be simple, even foolproof, it actually requires great skill. It is particularly important to have a definitive statement of what is to be figure and what is to be ground. Figure-ground-fusion decorating is not to the liking of everyone. Some people feel this kind of setting is psychologically distracting—"Too much is going on." Most people need the psychological and physical moorings of a high figure-ground organization.

Most people prefer well-defined figure-ground design in wall coverings. Geometric patterns and well-defined objects in patterns provide a more structured environment than free-floating abstracts. (These often take on Rorschach features into which one can read his own dynamics at any given time and so can be unsettling and even revealing.) However, too much structure of design and color suggests a rigid, inflexible orientation in either the designer or the occupant and might have such an effect on anyone in the area for a prolonged period.

The principle of *similarity* states that items (or people) that are similar in some way, or are assumed to belong together, have much in common. In the case of design, similar items are perceptually grouped. Thus a room of similarly shaped, covered, colored, or styled furniture or other decor will be perceived as grouped, however widely dispersed the items may be. Similar hues and/or degrees of brightness will be perceptually grouped. Similarity is an excellent device for handling large areas, because however widely dispersed the items may be, they are perceptually pulled together as a unit. Warm colors are grouped, as are cool colors and pastels. Pastels of the same hue are grouped with, or according to, the primary color to which they relate. Thus, a number of pieces of furniture in the same color will appear to be grouped even though they may be relatively far apart and dissimilar in style.

Continuity states that although there may be a variety of design themes, one overall design integrity or theme will retain its identity and dominate rather than be dominated by any minor themes. On the one hand, fractionated, atomized design and color schemes often tend to fractionate those who have to live and work among them; on the other hand, some breaks in continuity are essential to excitement. Therefore, a unified concept of color and/or design is to be recommended. This unity is achieved by defining a color scheme and then using variations on it. In the home or office, the principal color scheme should be established near the entrance; thereafter, as the person proceeds to other areas, he finds the same theme with new variations. For example, a red, white, and blue scheme can emphasize a red area with white and blue accents, a white area with red and blue accents, or a blue area with red and white accents. Another example is related to period: a modern idiom may remain modern throughout, although antiques and period items may be used. There may be a great shock value in giving each room a design and color entity of its own, but it will hardly be the most comfortable place to live.

Closure is the perceptual need for completion—to finish off, to see things (physically or psychologically) in terms of wholes. In design, closure is primarily a learned concept; for example, if we see a bridge table with three chairs, we look around for the fourth chair. A sofa with a chair at one end is perceived as an incomplete set if there is no chair at the other end. We look for units as a learned concept in design. On the other hand, there is a kind of physiological closure in the use of color. In a room of predominantly warm colors, we look for a cool color and vice versa. In fact, there is a tendency to become thirsty in a room of warm colors unrelieved by any cool colors.

In a room without color, a black-and-white room or a beige room, for example, the eye searches for color, any color. The need for color in human experience is exemplified by the fact that in experiments in which subjects are deprived of all color for a long period, they hallucinate color.

Generally speaking, the warm colors (red, yellow) tend to be figure, while the cool colors (green, blue, purple) tend to be ground. Black and white also are ground. Warm tones are "advancing colors," while cool colors are "receding." Thus the advancing colors are figure, the receding colors are ground; however, the specifics of color usage elude hard and fast formulas, and there can be many departures from these generalizations. For instance, following is a list of the eleven most visible color combinations. The order is figure on ground; that is, the first color given is the figure and the second is the ground.

yellow on black
white on blue
black on orange
black on yellow
orange on black
black on white
white on red
red on yellow
green on white
orange on white
red on green

It is important to note that brightness is a major factor in the determination of advancing or receding colors. A very bright cool color is advancing; a dull warm color is receding. Saturation is important for the same basic reasons. In conclusion, whether a color is advancing or receding depends on hue (warm advances, cool recedes), brightness (high advances, low recedes), and saturation (deep advances, shallow recedes).

There are other factors involved here, too. For instance, in the field of interior design, furniture, by its very nature, tends to become figure while walls and perhaps floor (covered or bare) tend to be ground. This "natural" relationship can be modified by the use of color, but it is a tricky business. Occasionally, when there are objects of special interest in the room—fine paintings, windows with spectacular views, pieces of sculpture— the furniture can be part of the ground if it is of a hue somewhat similar to the hue of the walls. It should not match the walls, however, since this would make for a room that is overbearingly monochromatic. Despite the truth of this principle, it is frequently ignored, and the results are boring. All too many settings fall into this trap. If this arrangement is used, the furniture can and should be spaced rather widely, so that one can see between and around the various pieces.

Depending on whether its color matches the wall or the furniture or neither, and depending on the degree of the match, the floor can be perceived as either figure or ground. A dark floor with pastel furniture and medium-hued walls would serve as a primary ground, with the walls as a secondary ground. Conversely, a light floor and wall with dark, loosely grouped furniture would serve as figure.

In a large area, if furniture color was similar to that of the walls and floor, and if the furniture was placed rather widely apart, the result would not be aesthetically pleasing. The figure-ground concept would be almost destroyed. A large area needs contrast, a strong figure-ground relationship. The trouble with the monochromatic room is that it lacks the contrasts the eye admires and the sensibilities require.

Furniture arrangement has become a lost art in an age when most homes are overfurnished. Some of the rooms one visits and sees pictured in magazines look like furniture showrooms, overcrowded and unplanned. The "togetherness' of furniture is important to an aesthetically pleasing arrangement, but this does not mean that chairs, sofas, and so on must be eyeball to eyeball.

The figure-ground method of designing lends itself to good furniture arrangement. It is not rigid or constricting, but is a highly fluid concept that often serves to eliminate potential errors. It might be argued that one man's figure is another man's ground, that it is all quite personal and tied up with the individual's perception of, and response to, different colors. While this is to some extent true, the integrity of the design, the fact that order has been established where chaos might have reigned, is paramount. And it makes a setting more interesting, too, when white furniture designed to serve as figure on a red-walled ground is perceived as white ground by someone whose favorite color is red. Figure-ground reversals are in fact common, and are all to the good.

In the planning of a figure-ground setting, the use of a model is superior to the use of sketches. The element of placement in a three-dimensional setting is particularly important in design according to figure-ground relationships.

In my consulting work I have used the concept of vectors and valences, which represents a kind of third-hand borrowing from the field of physics, where they represent physical energy force, via the field of psychology, where they represent forces of the mind and emotions. At any rate, in some of my work I have found it helpful to use these concepts to represent impulse-arousal merchandise and areas of merchandise.

One example of this work concerns the interior design of department stores. An obvious feature of the typical department store layout is its randomness. Most stores have the jewelry and perfume counters in close proximity on the first floor, but from there on arise wide discrepancies, based on little but chance.

Some stores have blouses and shoes on the main floor; others have dresses and coats. An assessment I made of the rationale for these layouts elicited a variety of responses. In one of my studies, I used the marketing-survey techniques of research and free association. In response to such merchandise cue words as shoes, lingerie, and so on, subjects were asked to respond with the first word or words that came to mind at the presentation of the stimulus word.

The results of these surveys were analyzed and "field valences" were charted. Valence is used here to represent the properties or values of a field that arouses tensions, needs, or forces (the vector). A valence is not an all-or-nothing thing; it can be weak, strong, or between the two extremes—the higher the concentration of items of similar impulse arousal, the stronger the field. The force (in this case, instinct) that propels one into action (buying) is the vector. However, the strength of the vector is related to the strength of the valence.

A field valence is the degree of impulse arousal of items on the scale from one to seven, and the grouping of those items that have a similar arousal value based on the hypothesis that, if items of similar value are grouped, the consumer would be "caught" in a "loaded" field; everywhere he turned, he would be met by another item that would satisfy the arousal need of that moment. Beyond this, the degree of arousal would be more intense and prolonged in this setting than in one where merchandise is arbitrarily or randomly scattered. In the latter, the shopper's need to purchase a greater number of items is diminished or even lost as he goes from one area to another.

For example, furs, shoes, hosiery, lingerie, and handbags represent a sex-field valence of the first or second magnitude and should represent an important grouping in our department store plan. Radiating out from these areas would be the items of lower rank in this particular set. Of course, there are still many field valence loadings other than those based on sex, and merchandise groupings could be effectively based on them, too. It is also important that negative valences not be included in a positive valence field. There is hardly any setting that can not have its valence charted for maximum effectiveness.

7/Applied color

Practically all of the color research conducted has been done by persons in the academic community and has had, as a basic goal, the better understanding of man in the physiological realms. However, North America is essentially a product- and service-oriented society, and it was inevitable that the results would find many practical applications. For example, one of the most persistent problems in the marketplace is how to determine which colors will be fashionable twelve to eighteen months hence, the time required to get the average product line—whether it be clothing, home furnishings or whatever—to the market. Before we examine some color research findings, it might be instructive to take a brief look at some significant color trends to see how color and historical forces have interacted.

The Victorian period was most depressing in terms of individual expression. Characterized by a repression of man's natural drives and the assumption of a facade of piety, purity, and morality, it was a time of hypocrisy. The literature of the period portrayed neurotic characters with repressed, unfulfilled needs and drives. (Freud's emphasis on sex and the instinct was probably an outgrowth of a societal bias in the opposite direction.) The principal colors of that period were murky shades of brown, red, lavender, and purple. The fabric samples of that period in the Forstman Museum have constricted, precise, rigid designs.

There was a brief flash of color in the period preceding World War I. The Russian Ballet was the rage of Paris and the rich colors of Imperial Russia, magenta, bright orange, and violet, became fashionable. Style leaders like Isadora Duncan adopted these colors for their private wardrobes. These colors did not sift down to the general public, however, perhaps because of the economic caution of the fabric manufacturers, or perhaps because there was not a democracy of taste as we know it today. This moment of gaiety fell before the impending gloom of World War I, when wearing khaki, tans, and grayish and olive greens became the fashionable way of life.

The so-called Roaring Twenties were everything but gay in color. Except for the introduction of red shoes, beige, gray, and a medium (Nordic) blue were the outstanding colors, with brown and a combination of navy blue and white close behind. Psychologists have generally attributed this rather colorless period to an emotional letdown after the prolonged tension of the war. There also existed a prejudice against the darker peoples at the time; consequently, the hot Mexican, Spanish, and Italian colors were unthinkable, except in fancy dress costumes. The Nordic blues remained popular until the 1950s.

The colors during the worldwide Depression of 1929-39 were the rich dark wines, bottle greens, and chocolate browns—colors that fostered feelings of security in this insecure age. These colors look murky to us today because of the brilliance of contemporary colors. The one concession to gaiety and

114

frivolity during this troubled period was the white and light accent.

In most countries, the years of World War II were drab and depressing, but there were some bursts of brightness, especially toward the end of the conflict, and in the United States, where many areas of the economy were extremely prosperous. However, just as the neutral beiges, tans, and grays were predominant after World War I, so were they again popular in 1946. The availability of dyes and color had nothing to do with this, as a great many new chemicals and the capacity to produce them had been developed during the war. Again, it was simply a period of high emotionalism and tension that was necessarily followed by a period in which neutral colors gained the ascendancy, reflecting an emotional tapering off after prolonged tension.

By 1948, the silhouette, as exemplified in the "new look" (the dropped hemline), appeared to be more important than color. The 1950s saw a gradual introduction of color—mostly pastels. These colors have generally been predominant in those periods when the female role, for better or for worse, has been strongest. The periods of the great courtesans, like Napoleon's Josephine, for instance, have been characterized by pastel colors.

The early 1960s saw the beginning of the color revolution, which paralleled the revolutions that were occurring in most other spheres of life. The old guidelines for color usage and color harmony became obsolete overnight, and a whole new generation of designers, artists, and colorists grew up with either ignorance of color harmony rules or total disregard of them.

The color revolution reflected the falling of barriers in various other areas, the release of energy (color is radiant energy, say some prophets), and the uninhibited drive of an increasingly young population. The election of President Kennedy and the focus on young leadership propelled a whole new segment of the population into action. The emergence of the African nations as world powers added to the momentum of the new forces at work. The world was energized, and the pressures of unchanneled energy broke new ground in many spheres of human existence.

No movement happens accidentally, but rather a movement is a response to the stresses and pressures of society, it is like the blow-out bubble on an automobile tire. The psychedelic movement in the early 1960s is no exception; it was in response to the pressures of an overly affluent, leisure oriented society in which traditions, values, and modes of life were in flux, a new political order flickered on the horizon, new nations were rising, the young were on the march—the world was energized.

The psychedelic phenomenon is defined as the merging of all stimuli—sound, touch, sight, and smell; visual imagery and color are its most significant features. The experience is said to be mind- and consciousness-expanding. A kind of kaleidoscopic play of color is experienced in the psychedelic state. Sounds are often translated into colors and vice versa. The psychedelic artists, followers, and practitioners played a role in the rise of neon bright colors, new color combinations, and heightened color-form awareness, by heeding and giving expression to the cues of the revolution and changes that were occurring worldwide during the 1960s.

While the makings of psychedelic experience have existed from the beginning of recorded time through the ingestion of certain plants, fasting, yoga, sensory deprivation, and so forth, the modern phase of the psychedelic movement is relatively new. It is dated from 1938, when the Swiss biologist Albert Hoffman discovered and synesthesized what he named lysergic acid diethylamide (LSD).

In the 1950s two Canadian scientists, Abram Hoffer and

Humphrey Osmond, who have worked extensively with a variety of mental patients, began working with LSD. In fact, Dr. Osmond, upon observing that subjects under the influence of LSD often seemed to discover new sensibilities and capabilities, coined the term "psychedelic." The age of psychochemistry took on momentum.[1]

However, the psychedelic movement was not totally drug-related; in fact, the psychedelic experience can be induced through the use of flashing, flowing, and changing bright colors and also through the combination of color, sound, abstract pattern and motion. The LSD, mescaline, peyote, psilocybin users were the exception and were called the hard-core psychedelics.

Out of the psychedelic movement has come an art movement that is unique in its coloration and content. Its artistic expression tends to be organic, molecular, cellular, and symbolic. It is concerned with both inward realities and also the reflection of external realities in a new dimension. There seems to be a primitive awareness in these artistic expressions of structures and materials (as reflected in symbolism and color) of civilizations long past, that now resides in man as biological and psychological "traces." Jung's archetypes and racial consciousness seem to have been tapped and brought to awareness. Some say that it is a forward thrust of the evolutionary process but one in which memory traces have been released from the archetypes and racial consciousness of Jungian constructs.[2] Others say that it is a forward thrust of the evolutionary process of man's spiritual nature.

To me psychedelic art and the other psychedelic expressions do not seem to be original creative expressions but rather reflections of the tensions, anxieties, and temperament of the times.

The psychedelic artists have generally tended to be of two types, those who were not drug oriented but who felt and

117

responded to the phenomenon, the movement, and those who were drug oriented and who tried to reproduce what they had seen under the influence of LSD. Neither seems to have produced a significant body of psychedelic art per se; however, the influence of the movement can be seen in a broad range of art, as well as in color and design expression in general.

Of course, no movement can forever remain at a white-hot stage, for unrelieved stress causes breakdowns in men and in systems. It is now obvious that color in the early 1970s is less strident than in the 1960s. Nevertheless, all revolutions leave their mark, and the old order has been irreversibly changed in the field of color.

For today's student of color, the revolution of the sixties, with its juxtaposition and acceptance of every possible color combination remains most important, for it called into re-examination all the rules that had previously dictated color usage, especially the law of complementary colors. The use of color complementaries as the only law of color planning and usage became obsolete overnight.

The concept of complementary colors is based on the color wheel, which is typically the placement of the primary and secondary colors in a circle in spectral order, that is, red, orange, yellow, green, blue, indigo, and violet. Those colors that are diametrically opposite each other on the circle are called complementary. Also, any combination of colors whose pigments yield a neutral gray-black when mixed together are called complementary. Another criterion of a complementary combination of colors is when one color is the afterimage of the other.

Afterimage is a physiological phenomenon whereby, after staring at a given color—say, red—for a few seconds, the individual "sees" the color opposite it on the color wheel—in this example, green. The physiological phenomenon of afterimage is used as "proof positive" by many persons working in the field of color that complementary colors are harmonious. As Itten states, "The principle of complementaries is the basis of harmonious design."[3] The physiological fact that the eye requires any given color to be balanced by its complementary, and will spontaneously generate it if it is not present, "proves the principle of color harmony implied in the rule of complementaries." Complementary colors are also those that meet without sharp contrasts, are similar in brightness, or are the same shade.

Other systematic variations of color relationships referred to as harmonious are split complementaries, triads, tetrads, hexads, and octads. Albers evaluates these concepts:

> Color terms which could be considered parallel to tone intervals are complementaries, split complementaries, triads, tetrads, and octads. Though these characterize distance and constellation within color systems, their definitions, such as incomplete triads and incomplete tetrads, indicate that their measure is only arbitrary. Significantly, complementaries . . . are topographically quite vague . . . . similarly, a triad or tetrad of one system will hardly fit into another system . . . . Illustrations of harmonic color constellations . . . are usually presented in a most theoretical and least practical manner . . . . Observe the interior and exterior, the furniture and textile decoration following such color schemes, as well as commercialized color "suggestions" for innumerable do-it-yourselfers. Our conclusion: we may forget for awhile those rules of thumb of complementaries, whether complete or "split," and of triads and tetrads as well. *They are worn out.* Second, no mechanical color system is flexible enough to precalculate the

> manifold changing factors, as named before, in a single prescribed recipe [italics mine].[4]

Not the least of these changing factors was the color explosion of the sixties that liberated color.

Furthermore, an examination of Itten's various harmonious color combinations reveals the weakness of his theory, for there are few, if any, color combinations that are not ultimately included in his harmonious system.

Triads

If three hues are selected from the color circle so that their positions form an equilateral triangle, those hues form a harmonious triad.

Yellow/red/blue is the clearest and most powerful of such triads . . . I should be inclined to call it the fundamental triad. The secondary colors, orange/blue-violet/yellow-green, are other triads whose arrangement in the color circle is an equilateral triangle.

Yellow-orange/red-violet/blue-green, or red-orange/blue-violet/yellow-green, are other triads whose arrangement in the color circle is an equilateral triangle.

If one color in the complementary dyad yellow/violet is replaced by its two neighbors, thus associating yellow with blue-violet and red-violet, or violet with yellow-green and yellow-orange, the resulting triads are likewise harmonious in character . . . .

Tetrads

If we choose two pairs of complementaries in the color circle whose connecting diameters are perpendicular to each other, we obtain a square . . . . The three tetrads of this kind in the 12-hue circle are:

> yellow / violet / red-orange / blue-green
> yellow-orange / blue-violet / red / green
> orange / blue / red-violet / yellow-green

More tetrads are obtained with a rectangle containing two complementary pairs:

> yellow-green / red-violet / yellow-orange /
> blue-violet; yellow / violet / orange / blue

A third geometrical figure for harmonious tetrads is the trapezoid. Two hues may be adjacent, and two opposing ones found to the right and left of their complements. The resulting chords tend to simultaneous modification, but they are harmonious; for when mixed, they produce gray-black.

By inscribing the polygons ... in a color sphere and rotating them, a very large number of further themes could be derived.

Hexads

Hexads may be derived in two different ways.

A hexagon, rather than a square or triangle, may be inscribed in the color circle. Three pairs of complementary colors are then obtained as a harmonious hexad. There are two such hexads in the 12-hue circle:

> yellow / violet / orange / blue / red / green
> yellow-orange / blue-violet / red-orange /
> blue-green / red-violet / yellow-green

This hexagon may be rotated in the color sphere. The resulting tints and shades yield interesting color combinations.

The other way to construct a hexad is to adjoin white and black to four pure colors. We place a square in the equilateral plane of the

> color sphere, obtaining a tetrad of two comple-
> mentary pairs. Then each vertex of the square
> is joined to white above and black below . . . .
> The result is a regular octahedron . . . .
> A rectangle may be used instead of a square;
> and an equilateral triangle combined with white
> and black yields pentads, such as yellow/red/
> blue/black/white or orange/violet/green/black/
> white, etc.[5]

The complementary-harmony school of colorists is based primarily on specific color systems or concepts, namely, the Munsell color system and Itten's color circle. Ostwald's color system, which uses a more subjective criterion of color harmony, is described by its creator as: "colors whose effect is pleasing, we call harmonious."[6] Harmony is in the eye of the beholder.

Opposites on the Ostwald color circle will neither mix into grays nor lend themselves to afterimages, but does this make the blue that is opposite the yellow that mixes into green on the Ostwald color circle any less harmonious than the blue that is opposite the orange on the Itten circle that mixes into gray?

Complementary colors equal harmony equals balance, according to the traditional school of colorists. Noncomplementary colors equal asymmetry equal tension, according to the modern school of colorists. But even these two frameworks do not take into consideration the eclectic approach, which utilizes neither of these orientations but, rather, is based on the demands of the space, subject matter, light, sequence of on-the-job applications and the colorist's interpretation of the overall tasks. The selection of colors within this framework does not concern itself with either complementary or noncomplementary colors. Indeed, as previously noted, a whole new generation of designers and colorists appears to have heard nothing of these rules. The increasing use of asymmetry in design and colors—in keeping with the tension, energy, and movement inherent with these concepts—is creating a new design idiom.

The concept of color harmony by the color wheel is an objective conclusion arrived at by intellectual activity. The response to color, on the other hand, is emotional; thus there is no guarantee that what is produced in a purely intellectual manner will be pleasing to the emotions. Man responds to form with his intellect and to color with his emotions; he can be said to survive by form and to live by color.

Albers feels that we should not hang onto the obsolete concept of color harmony. Instead, "in searching for new organization—color design—we have come to think that quantity, intensity, or weight as principles of study can lead similarly to illusions, to new relationships, to different measurements, to other systems, as do transparence, space, and intersection. Besides a balance through color harmony which is comparable to symmetry, there is equilibrium possible between color tensions, related to a more dynamic asymmetry."[7]

Disciples of the complementary color-harmony school support their theory by comparing it with consonance in music. This is, of course, like comparing fruit and nuts, and even if this were a valid comparison, the rise to prominence of such musical dissonants as Thelonious Monk and Cecil Taylor prove the validity of another system of music.

The reader should not get the impression here that "anything goes." There is certainly still good design and bad design; there is still effective use of color and poor use of color; there is still a vast gulf between good taste and bad taste. But the point of the color revolution was to get out from under the burden of all the old rules of good color usage that had been smothering genuine creativity. It takes a sharp, trained eye and skill and experience to create any kind of color environment appropriate to the needs of the particular situation. The goal of color usage is not always aesthetically pleasing either, taking into account such disparate factors as tension, excitement, manipulation, freedom, and expansiveness. The man who drips paint onto a canvas in a random manner may think that he is as good an artist as Jackson Pollock, but the critics and the informed public will probably reject his effort and rejoice in Pollock's creations.

The Greeks felt that "beauty consists in the . . . expression of unity and variety." Or, in terms of the discussion here, there is knowledge and plan behind a seemingly casual use of blue and green on an orange background. To work, such use of color must be well done, with a sense—partly learned and partly intuitive—of what is right and what is wrong for that particular situation. Those decorators and other colorists who learn one right and one wrong and then apply those principles to every environment are a throwback to the past. It follows that the practitioner of color would do well to make himself aware of what has been done in the field, particularly as far as the adducing of general principles and specific applications thereof and how they were arrived at.

To take an example of an attempt to quantify in art and related areas, in 1933 G. D. Birkhoff published his theory of aesthetic measure, which dealt with ornaments, vases, music, and poetry.[8] Ten years later, Moon and Spencer attempted to apply Birkhoff's theory to color harmony.[9] Aesthetic measure was defined by the equation $M = O/C$, where O represents the number of elements of order and C is the number of elements of complexity. While classical color harmony divides color combinations generally into two classes, harmonies and disharmonies, the system produced by the use of this equation is a continuous scale, from very poor to very good. In general, results followed Birkhoff's principle, "The simpler the palette is, the less will be the complexity, so that the palette should be as restricted as the subject permits. Evidently, the eye appreciates the repetition of a color, a graded sequence of colors, and a balance of light and dark values about the centers of interest."

There is, of course, a problem with this kind of measurement, and it is well expressed by Moon and Spencer: "There is the question of whether people with different degrees of color education will come to the same conclusion in rating a harmony." Of course, they won't. What was all the rage in the Gay Nineties will be virtually ignored in the Quiescent Fifties. The hottest color in the fashion centers of Europe may find a cool reception in the industrial centers of the American Middle West, although with improved devices of communication, such as color television, this wide gap may be somewhat narrowed.

Perhaps a more usable approach to the problem of color was put forth recently by Bernard Aaronson.[10] He asked a sample of 66 people, evenly divided between males and females, to rate eight conventional colors and three achromatic colors in light of the following adjectives: adventurous, affectionate, cautious, gloomy, impulsive, obedient, quarrelsome, resentful, self-conscious, shy, sociable, and sullen. The colors were red, orange, yellow, yellow-green, green, blue-green, blue, purple, white, gray, and black. The ratings for all colors except green were significantly different from chance. Red and orange were similar in triggering active, outgoing, rebellious, and assertive moods. Yellow was active without conflict. Yellow-green was seen in terms of outgoing conflict and aggression. Blue-green was outgoing, too, but calmer and socialized, which also characterized blue, though in a less outgoing way. Purple seemed associated with antisocial acting out. White has to do with obedience, gray with depression, and black with a kind of unhappiness that one is fighting, or at any rate that is not passive, as is gray. There are some sex differences: more males than females feel that orange and yellow imply conformity, that yellow-green and purple have positive values, that blue is negative, and that both white and black are active.

As an illustration of how color evaluations can change with different investigations, consider the study made by J. P. Guilford.[11] He said, "The greatest sex differences occur in reaction to the hues of red-purple, purple, and yellow-red. Greatest similarity between the sexes occurs in the region from yellow to blue." This, of course, is not in conformity with the results obtained by Aaronson, although it must be said that Guilford was not measuring anything more specific than the affective value of each color. Guilford also found an interesting sex difference: women are more sensitive to variations in hue than men. Another interesting point made by Guilford bears repeating here.

> [There is] growing freedom and increasing recognition of value in the employment of colors. Perhaps this is only one phase of the fact that our culture no longer frowns heavily upon sensory enjoyment, or of the fact that our civilization is now past the pioneer stages and our wealth and leisure foster attention to the arts as never before.

K. Warner Schaie has put forth three types of response to color: *unconditioned,* as when a bird responds to the color on the necks of her young; *conditioned,* as in the famous Pavlov experiments; and what might be called *reinforced.*[12] This latter, which is probably most important in man, can be characterized as an association that is not biologically necessary or organically conditioned but that has been operationally learned. To put these three categories into terms that are perhaps better

related to the practice of color, we can say that the unconditioned response is in the nature of a biological cue, a kind of
innate response, while the conditioned response is that which
is based on our environment: culture, family, age, and the like.
The color wheel is a conditioned response that has been arbitrarily imposed on man's loose system of color evaluation.

The question that remains to be answered is: What kind
of a response is it when a man is restless in an all-red room?
Guilford states that the affective value of color is directly
related to the brightness and saturation of the stimulus. Red is
red, whether you are an Eskimo, a pygmy, or a Texan. On the
other hand, Osgood et al. state "color preference is clearly
shown to be the result of learning, slow and arduous learning
at that."[13] There are as yet no definitive answers, but indications would seem to be that the intelligent practitioner will
take a little bit from both camps. Obviously, the very intensity
of a color, the physical length of its waves, is going to have a
definite effect on a person no matter what his background. Just
as obviously, there are going to be variations on this theme
because, as individuals and as members of cultural groups, we
have different backgrounds on which the same color stimulus
is going to produce different effects.

To return to our three modes of response, let us take the
third dimension, which is basically symbolic whether it is the
white of purity or the red of the traffic light. Every color is
known to have symbolic meaning, but there are many symbolic
systems, a fact that creates great difficulty in fashioning any
orderly interpretation because the different systems often pose
mutually contradictory explanations. While there are great
differences among the symbolic meanings assigned by various
systems to various colors, it must be pointed out that only rarely
do these meanings conflict with the biologically determined
affective attributes of a color. For instance, colors at the cool

end of the spectrum are never used to symbolize excitement, unrest, or related emotions.

It now seems desirable to consider various practical applications of color. Research on the effectiveness of color versus black-and-white advertising consistently reports the advantage of color. Starch analyzed 12 million inquiries drawn in by 8,200 ads in national magazines and found that: (1) position of an ad made little difference in its effectiveness; (2) color ads draw about half again as many inquiries as black and white; (3) large ads attract more inquiries than do small ones, as might be expected, but not in direct proportion to the size.[14] While Warner and Franzen found that color generally outweighed impact in interest value,[15] color does not seem to be significantly superior to black and white in the promotion of a new brand (in establishment of an association between product and trade name). On the other hand, they found that color ads help to enhance and maintain the image of known products. Attention is also called to skill in the use of color and the adaptability of the product to portrayal in black and white or color.

Reports show that color pulls more returns in direct mail than black and white. In one case, an order of effectiveness of papers was reported as yellow, goldenrod, blue, and cherry red. However, the data necessary for determining the statistical significance of the differences were not presented, and a study carefully conducted and analyzed by Dunlap does not support those findings.[16] Using yellow, blue and cherry red postcards, with white cards as the control color, Dunlap did a routine business mailing. He had observed that Paterson and Tinker stated that "brightness contrast" between the print used and the background for the print is the critical feature in legibility and speed of reading; consequently attention was given to these features.[17] Little difference was reported in brightness contrast between the white cards and the yellow cards, and between the blue cards and the cherry cards. The colors individually approached maximum chroma, or saturation; consequently the contrast of the print on the blue and the cherry cards was not as great as the contrast between the print and the other two colored cards. The yellow cards, at 50.7 percent, had the highest percentage of returns, with the rank order of return for the other cards at 46.1 percent for the blue, 40.8 percent for the white, and 38.6 percent for the cherry cards. However, a statistical analysis of these findings using chi square indicated no significant difference in response or "pull" due to color.

Several years ago I made several promotional mailings, yellow for the first mailing, blue for the second, white for the third, and pale green for the fourth. No significant differences in response were attributable to color; however, the yellow and the white mailings were made on a considerably higher quality paper with a better quality of printing and greater attention to such details as the careful selection of stamps, unusual logo design, and individual signatures. These mailings pulled 10 to 1 as compared to the blue and green mailings; consequently, it was concluded that elegance in terms of "packaging" was the critical factor in obtaining replies. To test these findings, white and yellow mailings were later sent out in the same manner as the blue and the pale green; true to expectation, there were no significant differences in pull.

In the area of food, it has been demonstrated that there are color-flavor associations due to experience with natural and processed food. Guilford and Smith used an 11 point hedonic scale, ranging from unpleasant to most pleasant, to assess the affective values of 316 different color specimens. With the dimensions of brightness and saturation held constant, preferences were lowest in the yellow and yellow-green region. In spite of an association between color and flavor, however, color is less important than taste, odor, size, texture, and setting.

Consequently, food is rarely chosen solely on the basis of color, although specific foods that are identified with specific colors are accepted or rejected according to their proximity to the expected color.[18]

Foster investigated the relationship between color association and flavor of food by having subjects evaluate speckled versus unspeckled dry snack products. The speckled sample was chosen significantly less often for flavor and appearance than was the unspeckled sample, although they were identical in every other respect.[19] However, in an experiment where consumers were asked which of the two charcoal grilled samples was preferred, a higher preference was expressed for the speckled sample which appeared grilled.

In a test of preferences in which Schutz found that, although subjects preferred an orange-colored orange juice to a yellow-colored juice, taste preferences were rated equal. On the other hand, he also found that the flavor rating of an inferior juice was raised when it was colored to resemble that of one of a higher quality; consequently, he concluded that "spurious conclusions about food preferences may be reached by considering color independently of flavor factors and colors can be experimentally manipulated to serve as standards of good quality."[20]

The influence of past acquaintance and exposure upon the color and taste of products was demonstrated in studies by both Dunker and by Kanig. Dunker noted that white chocolate was rated as tasting less like chocolate than the better known, more widely used brown product.[21] Kanig had 200 students of pharmacy identify by taste variously colored and flavored syrups. Flavorings presented in colorless syrups were generally incorrectly identified; there were even fewer correct identifications when the liquids were atypically colored.[22]

Further evidence of the widespread use and learning associated with the use of artificial colorings in food came in a study by Johnson, in which he demonstrated that preferred colors associated with flavor are not always those that are natural to the food. Examples used to demonstrate his point are that: (1) butter is artificially colored when natural carotene content is low; (2) if green coloring were not used, mint-flavored ice cream would be white; (3) the amount of orange color provided by natural orange juice is inadequate to meet the color expectation of orange sherbet.[23]

Pangborn studied the effect of food coloring on the sweetness and flavor of solutions of various concentrations of sucrose, citric acid, imitation flavoring, and artificial coloring in distilled water. Some differences were noted in the evaluation of trained and untrained subjects; specifically, the untrained had a slight tendency to "ascribe greater sweetness and greater flavor to orange- and red-colored solutions containing apricot and cherry flavoring, respectively, especially when sucrose differences were very small." The untrained were more accurate in their assessment of sweetness when color differences were masked with red illumination than were the trained, who showed a decrease in accuracy. A positional bias was noted for both groups in that there was a tendency to ascribe more sweetness and more flavor to the first sample within a group.[24]

Adding the dimensions of sourness and the color blue, Pangborn and Hansen did a follow-up study of sweetness. The uncolored nectar was correctly identified more frequently within pairs than colored nectars. Wide individual differences were manifested in color-taste associations for this group, with a tendency toward less accuracy in the identification of taste in colored than uncolored nectars. The investigators indicated "that visible variables interfered with gustatory responses."[25]

Pangborn, Berg, and Hansen studied the effect on discrimination of sweetness by coloring dry, white table wine. The results showed that, when sucrose level was held constant, white and pink wines were judged to the sweetest, while yellow, brown, red, and purple wines were judged to be less sweet. The experienced group was shown to be more influenced by the color variables than the naive group.[26] Ough and Amerine studied the color preferences in red wine according to sex, experience, and training and found that both the experienced and inexperienced groups preferred a red of middle brightness to orange and purple hues. Males showed a slight tendency to prefer a lower brightness level than females. A preference for decreasing brightness was indicated by the trained subjects. The over-dark purple wine was decidedly rejected by both the adult and student subjects, but the preference for this color was split for the experts. The investigators pointed out the dangers in using the preferences of a highly trained group to project the preferences of an inexperienced group.[27]

Stereotypes die hard, if at all. The resistance to giving up stereotypes may in part be attributable to the fact that they tend to represent exaggerated aspects and, hence, are easy to remember. They also tend to have humorous aspects. Not the least of the stereotypes is the dumb blonde—Clare Booth Luce and an assortment of other brainy blondes notwithstanding. Although Lawson's study found that natural blondes received higher ratings than artificial blondes on qualities such as beauty, intelligence, femininity, and the like, brunettes are perceived by both men and women as the stable, intelligent, valuable, strong, and sincere women.[28]

Specifically, using Semantic Differential ratings such as beautiful-ugly, entertaining-dull, strong-weak, dependable-undependable, unemotional-emotional, out of 21 pairs of adjectives, each hair color group except blondes and artificial blonde women (who rated blondes and brunettes evenly) rated its own hair color group highest. For example, dark men rated dark males highest, blonde men rated blonde males highest, and brunette women rated brunette women highest. Overall, men rated brunette females superior on 37 out of 63 possible comparisons, blondes on 17, redheads on 5, and artificial blondes on 2. Women rated brunettes significantly higher on 47 comparisons, blondes on 9, redheads on 8, and artificial blondes on 1.

M. N. Bartholet observed the use of color by pharmaceutical companies to reduce error on medication and the use of color by other industries to motivate improvements in employee morale, so he hypothesized that color might be able to motivate sick people to get well and might also improve nursing care.[29] Consequently, a study was conducted in which student nurses were requested to write down the first color associated with a list of words that fell into two categories, namely, those that pertained to the nurse's self-image, her image of other nurses, and those that pertained to the student nurse's perception of the patient.

The overall results indicated that while nurses seem to see themselves in an infinite variety of colors, patients are seen generally as "white, pink, blue, red, or a little green." The investigator raises the question as to whether or not all patients tend to seem alike to nurses.

In the association of white, nurses were seen as business-like, clean, cold, crisp, efficient, professional, and skillful. On the other hand, patients were seen at the other extreme as timid, passive, and scared. When related to themselves, the nurses viewed yellow as cheerful, optimistic, encouraging, and pleasant; as related to the patient, yellow was jaundice.

Orange was related to enthusiastic nurses and anxious patients; as a second choice, it was associated with difficult patients. Nurses saw themselves as pink—friendly, caring, nice, kind, and tender; patients who were docile, appreciative, grateful, healthy, and shy were associated with pink. Red, as a nursing-related color, was seen as bold, brassy, cruel, dominating, hasty, nosey, and sarcastic; red as a patient-related color was discomfort, aching, apprehensive, belligerent, distressed, cramping, touchy, stress, hot, and hurt.

Purple was self-associated with snobbery and patient-associated with dignity, sadness, sorrow, gravity, and regal power. Blue evoked a self-response that tended to be therapeutic and, conversely, as quite ill in relation to patients. Insincere and selfish were the self-associations with the color green, and nausea and sickness as patient-related (and to think of all those hospital walls painted "institutional green"). Gray words associated with nurses were condescending, indifferent, lazy, sloppy, and unfeeling. Patient-related gray meant bored, dependent, gloomy, inhibited, and worried. Black was professionally associated with bossy, critical, distrustful, hardboiled, rough, and uncaring; when black was associated with patients, it meant difficult and fearful.

The investigator concluded that from her research findings such recommendations as the following could be made:

(1) Large and frightening pieces of machinery should be painted the same as background colors to make them appear less obvious.
(2) Since green is most frequently associated with sickness and nausea, fewer rooms should be so painted.
(3) The white uniform should be reassessed.
(4) Increase or reinforce those colors that are most favorably associated. Colorful and good diets, attractive trays, attention to ceiling colors.
(5) Bright accents, such as a red water pitcher, might serve as a focal point during intake of medication.
(6) Since pink is the color of the favorite patient,

perhaps pink sheets could be added. Warm and soft colors in bedpans and other equipment should be considered.

In doing research into color preferences of a depressed group, I found that they had a strong preference for bright gay colors. This was not in line with the work of other investigators, who have found a preference among people of this type for dark neutral colors, grays, browns, and blacks; this preference has been attributed to the depressives' disinterest in the world around them. The depressives I worked with were withdrawn too, and their preference for bright primary, secondary, and tertiary colors seemed to me a compensatory reaction to the bleakness of their inner lives and/or an expression of a need for an energizing stimulus. While it is true that dark drab colors unquestionably reflect the mood of the depressive, it still seems not unusual to me that people of this type would want to get some color into their lives. Since I got the opposite color preference, a question arises in my mind as to the testing technique used by other investigators, especially as it relates to the subjects' understanding of the instructions. Severe depressives so turn off the world that they frequently do not fully understand test-taking procedures. Consequently, I made certain that my group fully understood my instructions. Hence, I feel my results are valid.

The depressive's preference for bright colors seems to me to reflect the homeostatic process whereby the organism is always striving for equilibrium. Bright colors, of course, would balance the slowed physiological process in response to the psychological process. While the concept of homeostasis is meant to be applied to the physiological processes, it is my conviction that there is a psychological homeostasis, too—if indeed, one can say that there is a difference between the psychological and physiological. I feel that they are one and the same and that when something goes wrong in a psychologically related physical process or organ, then psychological problems arise, and vice versa.

This kind of data could, of course, be effectively used in color planning the environments of depressive patients. In fact, I have thought of a psychiatrist's office in which there would be two sets of draperies: a red one to be drawn for the depressive patients, and a cool blue one for manic patients.

A study of the color preferences of older persons (90 people, aged sixty-five to eighty-nine) indicated that they prefer bright primary, secondary, and tertiary colors to the pale pastels. Thus, those who paint every institutional wall in drab or pastel colors are quite mistaken in their belief that old people like these "restful" colors. Also, misguided clothing manufacturers invariably make dresses for mature ladies in somber grays, blacks, and browns. This is unfortunate, as it has resulted in a kind of color starvation in this age group. This group also tends to perceive bright, deep colors lighter than they are perceived by younger age groups. I have hypothesized that, just as there is a dulling of taste buds in oldsters that results in the tendency to use too much salt in cooking, the changes that go on in the eye (yellowing, etc.) cause colors to be perceived less intensely than they ordinarily are. A nursing home for the aged should be decorated in a mixture of primary and pastel colors. Primary colors give the sense of security and stimulation needed by this group, and pastel colors serve to soften the overall effect. It would also be fun and amusing for both decorator and residents if supergraphics and other touches were added.

Persons of the lower socioeconomic groups, regardless of race, express a preference for bright strong colors. This would seem to be a direct result of the drabness of their surroundings. People caught in this kind of a trap try to break the monotony by having bright walls, clothing, and the like.

There is a story of a certain department store chain that built a gleaming black-and-white branch in one of the affluent, sophisticated northeastern suburbs. It became an outstanding success. Wishing to repeat this success, they put an almost exact duplicate of this store in another suburb, this one dominated by the homes of blue collar workers and their places of employment. Needless to say, it was an instant failure, not only because of the subtleties of the psychological preferences between these two groups, but also because of the dirt and soot and dust and general drabness that covered the houses and factories and clothing of everyone in the area. A pristine black and white store was obviously doomed here.

In years past, as people climbed up the social ladder or made money and achieved a higher status, they tended more and more to select pastels. One could thus conclude that with opportunity and advantage, a person's life was not so restricted and did not depend on immediate environmental stimuli. However, the shade and brightness of colors no longer distinguish social groups. With saturation affluence, even the rich are turning to bright, deep, strong colors more and more in their search for—what? Escape from boredom? Desire to be young? The results really are not in yet. The only thing we know is what we see: color, and plenty of it. Studies in California and Texas suggest that Westerners really do prefer bright sunny colors, colors that remind them of desert flowers. Perhaps it's the more open frame of mind one finds in the West, or maybe it's because one has to use bold, bright colors to make any kind of impression on that vast landscape.

Black is becoming a positive color with the young and early-middle-age people, both men and women. It is not a popular positive choice, but rather it has gone from a 100 percent negatively perceived color for decoration and popular usage to about 90 percent, a significant jump over a relatively short testing period. Men find black less negative than women do.

THE PSYCHOLOGY OF COLOR AND DESIGN

Too many colors in one setting are disconcerting, whether they are on a color preference sheet, in a room, or in a dress. Too many colors evoke incorrect responses to test questions, a higher than normal number of errors in arithmetic problems, and a general diffusiveness.

These and other principles operate in designing various color schemes. For example, when I began color planning department stores, designers incorrectly assumed that painting each wall in a different color reduced apparent space. In fact decorators and architects joined the designers in believing that large areas were broken up and made to appear smaller by the use of many colors.

However, my research has shown that large amounts of one color are more advancing, hence space reducing, than many colors in the same areas. The wrong use of a color scheme merely induces a feeling of randomness instead of focused buying in the customer. Consequently the multicolored, patchwork department store has disappeared.

The smaller, specialized areas in department stores had previously tended to be white, pale gray, or beige. The theory was that merchandise could be shown more advantageously against a neutral background. Art galleries operated on the same principle. But my department store color schemes have shown that merchandise can be as effectively displayed against one of any number of colors. In specialty shops and in art galleries we see any one of various colors.

The rise of supergraphics has been attributed to me. This art form did not grow out of a conscious effort on my part for artistic expression. If I have been instrumental in the popularity of supergraphics, it is because color has followed form.

This principle may be witnessed in the work I have done on race tracks, especially those that were highly skeletal, or little more than barns when I began. Since I am not a camouflage artist and since I believe that unattractive features should be accented or dramatized, I treated exposed beams, rafters, columns, studdings, and other structural details so that they became long, flowing sweeps of color.

The arrows I have doodled since childhood show up in my design work; so columns, stair rails, and beams become huge directional arrows that often run for hundreds of yards. Off-shoot arrows point out in intermediary directions.

Exposed ceiling features are often fused to the supporting columns by the use of color that sometimes gives the illusion of an umbrella-like framework out of a chaos of structural members. Most important of all are the bold, flowing lines and arrowheads that were widely written about in the press and so began a design expression that was soon to sweep the design magazines. This marked the end of the custom of painting exposed ceilings and other structural details black or gray in an effort to hide them.

The most important thing in the dramatization of these skeletal race tracks (or any job in which structural features are incorporated into the decor) is to maintain a certain amount of flow so that the overall impression will not be one of rigidity with endless straight and slanted lines.

Optimally three and certainly no more than four colors should be used in this type of planning otherwise the functional use of color will be lost in a crazy quilt of colors. Helter-skelter colors can affect the spatial and psychological orientation of the observers.

It is not necessary to use a neutral background. On the contrary, a background of any color may be used, the only condition being that the accented features be a sharp contrast of equal intensity if the background is deep or bright, or both.

Just as color follows form, design often follows a working title or working name. In the assessment of a color design job,

139

I have developed the technique of recording the cue-name that the business generates. Frequently this name bears no relation to the real name or to the owner's feeling about his establishment.

These cue-names aren't necessarily to be made public. A job I worked on once generated a rather risque working title which I placed on the working sheets. Unfortunately I left these sheets on the job overnight. The president of that dignified, tradition-bound, pillar of American business company did not exactly appreciate the source of my artistic inspiration.

Working titles do generate color as well as design and image cues at the most basic, visceral level. The designer can thus get beyond his preconceived notions regarding a job. Cookie-cutter designing is eliminated. A working title and design cues individualize the job and foster image projection which is the goal of a color and design job in business.

Finally, I would like to make a long, overdue correction of M. E. Chevruel's graduated scale of grays. Since the mid-1800s Chevruel's theory of color has been taught in art and design schools, and his thinking continues to be talked and written about by people apparently oblivious to the fact that there is not a one-to-one ratio between a physical stimulus and the resulting conscious sensation.[30]

Years ago I ran across an excellent illustration of the errors in Chevruel. In *Interaction of Color* Josef Albers quotes Chevruel's directions for obtaining a graduated scale of grays:

> Upon a sheet of cardboard divided into ten stripes, each about a quarter of an inch broad, lay a uniform tint of India ink. As soon as it is dry, lay a second tint on all the stripes except the first. As soon as the second is dry, lay a third one on all the stripes except the first and second,

and so on all the rest, so as to have ten flat tints
gradually increasing in depth from the first to
the last.

If one were to follow these directions, he would be in
for a surprise: the gradual "increase in depth" does not occur
psychologically.

Analysis of Chevruel's method reveals there is "not only
an additive mixture with regard to color, but also a subtractive
mixture with regard to light."[31]

How do you then bring about a visually even progression
in mixture? Albers finds the answer in the Weber-Fechner
Law: The visual perception of an arithmetical progression
depends upon a physical geometric progression.[32]

To understand "this surprising discrepancy between physical fact and psychic effect," the reader is referred to the dia-
grams given and experiments suggested in Albers.

If there is one single conclusion to be drawn from the
ideas discussed in this chapter, it is that those of us who work
with color and design, if we are to work most effectively, must
have an understanding of both the psychical and physical
worlds.

Notes

Notes: Preface

1. E. Schachtel, "On Color and Affect: Contributions to an Understanding of Rorschach's Test," *Psychiatry* 6 (1943): 393-409.

2. Maria Rickers-Ovsiankina, "Some Theoretical Considerations Regarding the Rorschach Method," *Rorschach Research Exchange* 7 (1943): 741-53.

3. K. Warner Schaie and R. Heiss, *Color and Personality* (New York: Grune & Stratton, 1963).

Notes: Chapter 1

1. J. W. von Goethe, *Farbenlehre* (Weimar, 1810).

2. M. E. Chevreul, *The Principles of Harmony and Contrast of Color and Their Applications to the Arts,* based on the first English edition of 1854 as translated from the first French edition of 1839 (New York: Reinhold Publishing Corp., 1967).

3. Gustav J. von Allesch, "Die Aesthetische Erscheinungsweise der Farbe," *Psychologische Forschung* 6 (1925):1-91.

4. Albert H. Munsell, *A Color Notation* (Baltimore: Munsell Color Co., 1941).

5. Wilhelm Ostwald, *Color Science* (London: James Walker, 1931, 1933).

6. J. P. Guilford, "A Study in Psychodynamics," *Psychometrika* 4 (1939): 1023.

7. Edward Bullough, "The Perceptive Problem in the Aesthetic Appreciation of Single Colours," *British Journal of Psychology* 2 (1908): 406-63.

8. Albert R. Chandler, *Beauty and Human Nature* (New York: D. Appleton-Century Co., 1934).

9. Harry Helson, "Adaptation Level Theory," *Psychology,* ed. Sigmund Koch (New York: McGraw-Hill, 1959).

Notes: Chapter 2

1. Anthony F. Gramza and Peter A. Witt, "Choices of Colors among Preschool Children," 29 (1969): 783-87.

2. K. Warner Schaie, "Developmental Changes in Response Presentation on a Color Arrangement Task," *Journal of Consulting and Clinical Psychology* 32 (1968): 233-35.

3. Pavel Machotka, "Aesthetic Criteria in Childhood" (Ph.D. dissertation, Harvard University, 1962).

4. See Jean Piaget, *The Origins of Intelligence in Children,* trans. Margaret Cook (New York: Basic Books, 1952).

5. R. Alschuler and L. Hattwick, *Painting and Personality* (Chicago: University of Chicago Press, 1947).

6. Lenore Adler, "A Note on Cross-Cultural Preferences," *Journal of Psychology* 65 (1967): 15-22.

7. Joan A. Chase, "Color Preference on the Lowenfeld Mosaic Test: Position Influence," *Journal of Genetic Psychology* 106 (1965): 256-63.

8. Irvin L. Child, Jens A. Hansen, and Frederick W. Hornbeck, "Age and Sex Difference in Children's Color Preferences," *Child Development* 39 (1968): 237-47.

9. J. Salvia and J. Shugerts, "Color-Related Behavior of Mentally Retarded Children with Color Blindness and Normal Color Vision," *Exceptional Children* 37, no. 1 (1970): 37-38.

10. H. Rudsill, "Children's Preferences for Color vs. Other Qualities in Illustrations," *Elementary School Journal* 53 (1951): 444-51.

11. Lenore Adler, "The 'Fruit Tree Experiment' as a Measure of Children's Preferences of Fruit Trees under Varied Conditions of Color Availability," *Journal of Genetic Psychology* 116 (1970): 191-95, and "The 'Fruit Tree Experiment' as a Measure of Retarded Children's Preferences of Fruit Trees under Varied Conditions of Color Availability," *Journal of Psychology* 76 (1970): 217-22.

12. A. Bannatyne, "The Color Phonics System," in *The Disabled Reader: Education of the Dysteric Child,* ed. John Money and Gilbert Schiffman (Baltimore: John Hopkins University Press, 1966).

13. Caleb Gattegno, *Words in Color* (Reading, England: Educational Explorers, 1963).

14. C. W. Crannell, "Code Learning and Color," *Journal of Psychology* 58 (1964): 293-99.

15. Iri B. Krause and Isabella D. Thomas, "The Use of Colour Contextual Cues in Reading," *Slow Learning Child: The Australian Journal on the Education of Backward Children* 16, no. 1 (1969): 44-50.

16. W. Goldfarb and B. Klopfer, "Rorschach Characteristics of 'Institution Children,' " *Rorschach Research Exchange* 8 (1944): 92-100.

17. R. H. Fortier, "The Response to Color and Ego Func-

tions," *Psychological Bulletin* 20, no. 1 (1953): 41-63.

18. Hermann Rorschach, in *Journal of General Psychology* 27 (1942): 119.

19. M. Monnier, "The Rorschach Psychological Test," *Encephale* 29 (1934): 189-201, 247-70.

20. M. Monnier, "The Present Technique of the Rorschach Psychodiagnostic Test, Revision and Criticism," *Annales Medico-Psychologiques* 96 (1938): 15-22.

21. J. L. Endacott, "The Results of 100 Male Juvenile Delinquents on the Rorschach Ink-blot Test," *Journal of Criminal Psychopathology* 3 (1941): 41-50.

22. M. R. Hertz and E. Baker, "Personality Patterns in Adolescence as Portrayed by the Rorschach Ink-Blot Method: The Color Factors," *Journal of General Psychology* 28 (1943): 3-61.

23. P. Boynton and B. Wadsworth, "Emotionality Test Scores of Delinquent and Non-delinquent Girls," *Journal of Abnormal Psychology* 38 (1943): 87-92.

24. Fortier, "Response to Color," pp. 41-63.

25. E. Phillips and E. Stromberg, "A Comparative Study of Fingerpainting Performance in Detention Homes and among High School Pupils," *Journal of Psychology* 26 (1948): 507-15.

26. Fortier, "Response to Color," pp. 41-63.

Notes: Chapter 3

1. Martin Lindauer, "Color Preferences among the Flags of the World," *Perceptual and Motor Skills* 29 (1969): 892-94.

2. R. H. Knapp, "N Achievement and Aesthetic Preference," in *Motives in Fantasy, Action, and Society,* ed. J. W. Atkinson (Princeton, N.J.: Princeton University Press, 1958).

3. D. C. McClelland, *The Achieving Society* (New York: Free Press, 1961).

4. Lindauer, "Color Preferences," p. 894.

5. A. Chongourian, "Color Preferences and Cultural Variation," *Perceptual and Motor Skills* 26 (1968): 1203-6.

6. A. Chongourian, "Color Preferences: A Cross-Cultural and Cross-sectional Study," *Perceptual and Motor Skills* 28 (1969): 801-2.

7. C. E. Osgood, G. J. Suci, and P. H. Tannenbaum, *The Measurement of Meaning* (Urbana, Ill.: University of Illinois Press, 1957).

8. Lawrence Roderick Schall, "The Influence of the Expressive Meanings of Color on Form, Interpreted in Terms of a Sensory-Tonic Theory of Perception," (Ph.D. dissertation, University of Indiana, 1970). The material in this paper has been of the utmost help in preparing the explanation of the SD, for the purposes of this book, as it relates to color preferences.

9. W. T. Tucker, "Experiments in Aesthetic Communications" (Ph.D. dissertation, University of Illinois, 1955).

10. M. S. Miron, "A Cross-Linguistic Investigation of Phonetic Symbolism," *Journal of Abnormal Psychology* 62 (1961): 623-30.

11. Y. Tanaka, T. Oyama, and C. E. Osgood, "A Cross-Culture and Cross-Concept Study of the Generality of Semantic Spaces," *Journal of Verbal Learning and Verbal Behavior* 25/6 (1963): 392-405.

12. T. Oyama, Y. Tanaka, and Y. Chiba, "Affective Dimensions of Color: A Cross-Cultural Study," *Japanese Psychological Research* 4, no. 2 (1962): 78-91.

13. Ibid.

14. J. E. Williams, "Individual Differences in Color-Name Connotations as Related to Measures of Racial Attitude," *Perceptual and Motor Skills* 29 (1969): 383-86.

15. Albert J. Kastl and Irvin L. Child, "Comparison of Color Preferences in Vietnam and the United States," *Proceedings of the American Psychological Association, 1968*.

16. R. Serpell, "Cultural Influence on Attentional Prefer-

ence for Colour over Form" (Report of the Human Development Research Unit, University of Zambia, 1968).

17. T. Kellagham, "The Study of Cognition in a Non-Western Culture, with Special Reference to the Yoruba of Southwestern Nigeria" (Ph.D. dissertation, Queen's University, Belfast, 1965).

18. M. H. Irwin and D. H. McLaughlin, "Ability and Preference in Category Sorting by Mano Schoolchildren and Adults," *Journal of Social Psychology* 82 (1970): 15-24.

19. Earl Ogletree, "Skin Color Preferences of the Negro Child," *Journal of Social Psychology* 79 (1969): 143-44.

20. Kenneth Clark, *Prejudice and Your Child* (Boston: Beacon Press, 1963), pp. 46-47.

21. Irwin D. Glick, "An Investigation of the Effects of the Meta-Message of Skin Color and Neutral and Affective Language" (Ph.D. dissertation, University of Maryland, 1969).

22. J. E. Williams and C. A. Renninger, "Black-White Color Connotations and Racial Awareness in Preschool Children," *Perceptual and Motor Skills* 22 (1966): 771-85.

23. J. K. Morland, "Racial Recognition in Nursery School Children in Lynchburg, Virginia," *Social Forces* 37 (1958): 132-37.

24. J. K. Morland, "Racial Appearance and Preference of Nursery School Children in a Southern City," *Merrill-Palmer Quarterly of Behavior and Development* 8 (1962): 271-80.

25. C. Winick, "Taboo and Disapproved Colors and Symbols in Various Foreign Countries," *Journal of Social Psychology* 59 (1963): 561-68.

26. Ibid.

Notes: Chapter 4

1. K. L. Kelly and D. B. Judd, *The ISCC-NBS Method of Designating Colors and a Dictionary of Color Names* (National

Bureau of Standards Circular 553. Washington, D. C., 1955).

2. Alphonse Chapanis, "Color Names for Color Space," *American Scientist* 53, no. 3 (1965): 327-45.

3. J. P. Guilford and Patricia C. Smith, "A System of Color Preferences," *American Journal of Psychology* 62 (1959): 487-502.

4. J. P. Guilford, "There Is System in Color Preferences," *Optical Society of America Journal* 30 (1940: 455-59.

5. K. Goldstein, *The Organism* (New York: American Book Co., 1939).

6. C. O. Lawler and E. E. Lawler, "Color-Mood Associations in Young Children," *Journal of Genetic Psychology* 107 (1965): 29-32.

7. Max Pfister, "Der Farbpyramidentest," *Psychological Research* 1 (1950): 192-94.

8. K. Warner Schaie, "The Color Pyramid Test: A Nonverbal Technique for Personality Assessment," *Psychological Bulletin* 60, no. 6 (1963): 530-47, and Schaie and R. Heiss. *Color and Personality* (New York: Grune & Stratton, 1963).

9. M. Luscher, *The Luscher Color Test,* ed. Ian Scott (New York: Random House, 1965).

10. I. A. Berg, "Response Bias and Personality: The Deviation Hypothesis," *Journal of Psychology* 40 (1955): 60-71.

11. M. Sherif and H. Cantril, "The Psychology of Attitudes," *Psychological Review* 52 (1945): 309.

12. D. T. Sharpe, "A Study of Response Set as a Personality Variable" (Ph.D. dissertation, New York University, 1963).

13. M. J. Asch, "Negative Response Bias and Personality Adjustment," *Journal of Counseling Psychology* 5 (1958): 207.

14. A. Couch and L. Kenniston, "Yea-sayers and Naysayers: Agreeing Response Set as a Personality Variable," *Journal of Abnormal and Social Psychology* 60 (1960): 151-74.

15. C. W. Grant, "The Relation of Subtle Items and Response Bias to Measured Patterns of Personality (Ph.D.

dissertation, University of Minnesota, 1950).

16. A. L. Edwards, *Edwards Personal Preference Schedule*, rev. ed. (New York: Psychological Corp., 1959).

17. Hermann Rorschach, *Psychodiagnostik,* trans. P. Lemkau and B. Kronenberg (New York, Grune & Stratton, 1942).

18. R. Heiss, "Der Farbpyramidentest" (The Color Pyramid Test), *Psychological Research* 3 (1952): 1-41.

19. K. Warner Schaie, "Developmental Changes in Response Differentiation on a Color Arrangement Task," *Journal of Consulting and Clinical Psychology* 32, no. 2 (1968): 233-35.

20. R. H. Knapp, "N Achievement and Aesthetic Preference," in *Motives in Fantasy, Action, and Society,* ed. J. W. Atkinson (Princeton, N.J.: Princeton University Press, 1958), pp. 367-72.

21. D. C. McClelland, *The Achieving Society* (New York: Free Press, 1961).

22. S. Honkavaara, "Comparison of the Relation of Color and Form-Reactors at Harvard and Yale University," *Journal of Psychology* 46 (1958): 23-24.

23. S. Honkavaara, "The Accuracy of Perception in Relation to Interpersonal Relationships," *Journal of Psychology* 46 (1958): 19-21.

24. S. Honkavaara, "Relation of Interpersonal Preference and Emotional Attitude of the Subjects," *Journal of Psychology* 46 (1958): 25-31.

25. A. Bjerstadt, "Warm-Cool Color Preference as Potential Personality Indicators: Preliminary Note," *Perceptual and Motor Skills* 10 (1960): 31-34.

26. R. R. Crane and B. I. Levy, "Color Scales in Responses to Emotionally Laden Situations," *Journal of Consulting and Clinical Psychology* 26 (1962): 516-19.

27. Norma H. Compton, *Compton Fabric Preference Test*

(Agricultural Experiment Station, Utah State University, 1965).

28. Norma H. Compton, "Body Build, Clothing, and Delinquent Behavior," *Journal of Home Economics* 59, no. 8 (1967): 655-59.

29. S. Fisher and S. Cleveland, "Body-Image Boundaries and Style of Life," *Journal of Abnormal Psychology* 52 (1956): 373-79.

30. A. Petrie, R. McCulloch, and P. Kadzin, "The Perceptual Characteristics of Juvenile Delinquents," *Journal of Nervous and Mental Diseases* 134 (1962): 415-421.

31. Ibid.

32. B. I. Murstein, "The Stimulus," in his *Handbook of Projective Techniques* (New York: Basic Books, 1965).

33. Kay Chi Yu, "Differences in the Usage of Colors between Schizophrenics and Normals," *Acta Psychologica Taiwanica* 6 (1964): 71-79.

34. A. I. Pevzener, First Moscow Medical Institute, U.S.S.R., "On Disturbance of Color Vision in Schizophrenics," *Zhurnal Nevropatologii Psikhiatrii Im* 69, no. 1 (1969): 83-87.

35. A. Tolor, "A Preliminary Report Designed to Differentiate Patients and Cerebral Pathology and Osychoneurosis," *Journal of Clinical Psychology* 10 (1954): 43-47.

36. A Tolor, "A Re-evaluation of the Color Drawing Test," *Journal of Clinical Psychology* 14 (1958): 172-74.

37. E. H. Wig and L. S. Bliss, "Selections of Visual Dimensions by Aphasics and Non-aphasics," *Perceptual and Motor Skills* 31 (1970): 435-40.

38. E. Heidbreder, "The Attainment of Concepts, III: The Process," *Journal of Psychology* 24 (1947): 93-138.

39. P. Dale, "Children's Color Categories and the Problem of Language and Cognition," in *Studies in Language and Language Behavior,* ed J. C. Catford, CRLLB, Progress Report no. 6 (Ann Arbor, Mich. 1968)

40. C. Hall, "What People Dream About," *Scientific American* 184 (1951): 60-63.

41. P. H. Knapp, "Sensory Impressions in Dreams," *Psychoanalytic Quarterly* 25 (1956): 325-47.

42. W. S. Monroe, "Experiment in Dreams," *American Journal of Psychology* 9 (1897): 413.

43. E. Kahn, W. Dement, C. Fisher, and J. E. Barnard, "Incidence of Color in Immediately Recalled Dreams," *Science* 137 (1962): 1054-5.

44. J. W. Lovett Doust, "Studies in Physiology of Awareness. The Incidence and Content of Dream Patterns and Their Relationship to Neurosis," *Journal of Mental Science* 97 (1951): 801-11.

45. R. Husband, "Sex Differences in Dream Contents," *Journal of Abnormal and Social Psychology* 30 (1936): 513-21.

46. Hall, "What People Dream," p. 60.

47. Sigmund Freud, *The Interpretation of Dreams* (London: George Allen & Unwin, 1937), p. 389.

48. P. Greenacre, "Vision, Headache, and the Halo," *Psychoanalytic Quarterly* 16 (1947): 177-94.

49. V. Calef, "Color in Dreams," *Journal of the American Psychological Association* 2 (1954): 453-61.

50. P. H. Knapp, "Sensory Impressions in Dreams," *Psychoanalytic Quarterly* 33 (1964): 325-47.

51. R. Yazmajian, "Color in Dreams," *Psychoanalytic Quarterly* 33 (1964): 176-93.

52. R. M. Suinn, "Jungian Personality Typology and Color Dreaming," *Psychiatric Quarterly* 40, no. 4 (1966): 659-65.

53. Husband, "Sex Differences in Dream Content," pp. 513-21.

54. W. C. Middleton, "The Frequency with Which a Group of Unselected College Students Experience Colored Dreaming and Colored Hearing," *Journal of General Psychology* 27 (1942): 221-29.

55. H. R. Blank, "Dreams of the Blind," *Psychoanalytic Quarterly* 27 (1958): 158-74.

Notes: Chapter 5

1. Gerda Smets, "Time Expression of Red and Blue," *Perceptual and Motor Skills* 29 (1969): 511-14.

2. G. D. Wilson, "Arousal Properties of Red Versus Green," *Perceptual and Motor Skills* 23 (1966): 947-49.

3. B. B. Brown, "Recognition of Aspects of Consciousness through Association with EEG Alpha Activity Represented by a Light Signal," *Psychophysiology* 6, no. 4 (1970): 442-52.

4. B. B. Brown, "Recognition of Associations between Aspects of Consciousness and EEG Frequencies Using Colored Lights Operated by Specific EEG Components," *Psychophysiology* 5 (1969): 574.

5. As reported by John A. Osmundsen, *New York Times,* 29 Nov. 1964, p. 80, col. 6.

6. K. Goldstein, "Some Experimental Observations: The Influence of Colors on the Functions of the Organism," *Occupational Therapy* 2 (1942): 147-51.

7. R. Gerard, "The Differential Effects of Colored Lights on Physiological Functions" (Ph.D. dissertation, University of California at Los Angeles, 1957).

8. J. S. Nakshian, "The Effect of Red and Green Surroundings on Behavior," *Journal of General Psychology* 70 (1964): 145-61.

9. L. Halpern and S. Kugelmass, "The Variability of Reaction Time in the Sensorimotor Induction Syndrome with Special Reference to the Effect of Colors," *Journal of Psychology* 41 (1956): 225-69.

10. W. T. James and W. R. Domingos, "The Effect of Color Shock on Motor Performance and Tremor," *Journal of General Psychology* 48 (1953): 187-93.

11. As reported in John E. Gibson, "How Well Do You Understand People?" *Today's Health,* March 1967, pp. 28-29.

12. M. L. Rubin, "Spectral Hue: Loci of Normal and Anomalous Trichromates," *American Journal of Ophthalmology* 52 (1961): 166.

13. W. Richards, "Differences among Color Normals," *Optical Society of America Journal* 57, no. 8 (1967): 1047-55.

14. G. H. M. Waaler, "Heredity and Two Normal Types of Color Vision," *Nature* 218 (1968): 688-89.

15. D. Katz, *The World of Color* (London: Paul, Trench, Trubner, 1935).

16. K. Grunewald and K. Hapten, "On Gestalt Psychology as a Clue to a Possible Source of Error in Examination of the Color Sense," *Acta Ophthalmologica* 32 (1954): 425-29.

17. H. L. White and A. C. Price, "Figure-Ground Confusion on a Test for Color," *Perceptual and Motor Skills* 11 (1960): 131-36.

18. J. G. Gilbert, "Age Changes in Color Matching," *Journal of Gerontology* 12 (1957): 210-15, and Alphonse Chapanis, "A Relationship between Age, Visual Acuity, and Color Vision," *Human Biology* 22 (1950): 1-33.

19. J. C. Wheeler, "A Practical Knowledge of Color for the Congenitally Blind," *New Outlook for the Blind* 63, no. 8 (1969): 225 ff.

20. Ibid.

21. *Time,* 25 Jan. 1963, p. 47.

22. R. P. Youtz, "The Case for Skin Sensitivity to Color With a Testable Explanatory Hypothesis" (Paper read at Psychonomic Society Meeting, Niagara Falls, N.Y., October, 1964). See also letter, *Scientific American* 212 (1965): 8-9.

23. R. B. Barnes, "Thermography of the Human Skin," *Science* 140 (1963): 870-77.

24. J. D. Hardy and C. Muschenheim, "Radiation of Heat

from the Human Body," *Journal of Clinical Investigation* 15 (1936): 1-9.

25. T. W. Oppel and J. D. Hardy, "Studies in Temperature Sensation," *Journal of Clinical Investigation* 16 (1937): 517-40.

26. R. Buckhout, "The Blind Fingers," *Perceptual and Motor Skills* 20 (1965): 191-94.

27. W. L. Makous, "Cutaneous Color Sensitivity," *Psychological Review* 73, no. 4 (1966): 280-94.

28. C. D. Hodgman, R. C. Weast, and S. M. Selby, eds., *Handbook of Chemistry and Physics,* 42nd ed. (Cleveland: Chemical Rubber, 1960).

29. A. Zavala, H. P. Van Cott, D. B. Orr, and V. H. Small, "Human Dermo-optical Perception: Colors of Objects and of Projected Light Differentiated with Fingers," *Perceptual and Motor Skills* 25 (1967): 525-42.

30. C. M. Diserens, *The Influence of Music on Behavior* (Princeton, N.J.: Princeton University Press, 1926).

31. E. L. Mudge, "The Common Synaesthesia," *Journal of Applied Psychology* 4 (1920): 342-45.

32. K. Singer, *Diseases of the Musical Profession* (New York: Greenberg, 1932), p. 235.

33. J. E. Downey, "A Case of Colored Gustation," *American Journal of Psychology* 22 (1911): 528-39.

34. An unpublished experiment.

Notes: Chapter 6

1. Kurt Lewin, *Principles of Topological Research* (New York: McGraw-Hill Book Co., 1936).

2. Max Wertheimer, "Untersuchungen zur Lehre von der Gestalt," *Psychologische Forschung* 1 (1922): 47-58; portions trans. in *A Sourcebook of Gestalt Psychology,* ed. W. D. Ellis (New York: Harcourt, Brace and World, 1938).

3. E. R. Hilgard, *Introduction to Psychology* (New York: Harcourt, Brace and World, 1962), p. 193.

Notes: Chapter 7

1. Abram Hoffer and Humphrey Osmond, *Hallucinogens* (New York: Academic Press, 1967).
2. C. G. Jung, *Man and His Symbols* (Garden City, N.Y.: Doubleday, 1964).
3. Johannes Itten, *The Art of Color* (New York: Rheinhold Publishing Corp., 1961), pp. 118-119.
4. Josef Albers, *Interaction of Color* (New Haven, Conn.: Yale University Press, 1971), pp. 41-42.
5. Itten, *Art of Color,* pp. 115-19.
6. Wilhelm Ostwald, *Color Science* (London, 1931, 1933).
7. Albers, *Interaction,* p. 42.
8. George D. Birkhoff, *Aesthetic Measure* (Cambridge, Mass.: Harvard University Press, 1933).
9. Parry Moon and Domina Spencer, "Aesthetic Measure Applied to Color Harmony," *Optical Society of America Journal* 34, no. 4 (1944): 234-39.
10. Bernard Aaronson, "Some Affective Stereotypes of Color," *International Journal of Symbology* 2, no. 2 (1970): 15-27.
11. J. P. Guilford, "The Affective Value of Color as a Function of Hue, Tint, and Chroma," *Journal of Experimental Psychology* 17 (1934): 342-70.
12. K. Warner Schaie, correspondence with author.
13. C. E. Osgood, G. J. Suci, and P. H. Tannenbaum, *The Measurement of Meaning* (Urbana, Ill.: University of Illinois Press 1957).

14. Daniel Starch, "How Size, Color, Position, and Location Affect Inquiries," and "How Types of Offers, Products, and Coupons Affect Inquiries," *Media Scope* 3, nos. 1-3 (1959): 23, 38, 40.

15. L. Warner and R. Franzen, "Values of Color in Advertising," *Journal of Applied Psychology* 31 (1947): 260-70.

16. W. J. Dunlap, "The Effect of Color in Direct-Mail Advertising," *Journal of Applied Psychology* 3 (1950): 280-81.

17. D. G. Paterson and M. A. Tinker, *How to Make Type Readable* (New York: Harper & Bros., 1940), pp. 118-29.

18. J. P. Guilford and P. C. Smith, "A System of Color Preferences," *American Journal of Psychology* 72 (1959): 487-502.

19. D. Foster, "Psychological Aspects of Food Colors from the Consumer Standpoint." (Mimeographed report from U.S. Testing Co., Hoboken, N. J., 1965.)

20. H. G. Schutz, "Color in Relation to Food Preferences," *Color in Foods: A Symposium,* reported in R. M. Pangborn, "Influence of Color and the Discrimination of Sweetness," *American Journal of Psychology* 73 (1960): 229-38.

21. K. Dunker, "The Influence of Past Experience upon Perceptual Properties," *American Journal of Psychology* 52 (1939): 263.

22. J. L. Kanig, "Mental Impact of Colors in Food Studied," *Food Field Reporter* 19 (1955): 23, 27.

23. A. H. Johnson, "Significance of Color in Dairy Products." (Mimeographed report from National Dairy Research Lab, Oakdale, N. Y., 1956), p. 33.

24. Pangborn, "Influence of Color," pp. 229-38.

25. R. M. Pangborn and B. Hansen, "The Influence of Color and Discrimination of Sweetness and Sourness in Pear Nectar," *American Journal of Psychology* 76 (1963): 315-17.

26. R. M. Pangborn, H. W. Berg, and B. Hansen, "The Influence of Color on Discrimination of Sweetness in Dry Table Wine," *American Journal of Psychology* 76 (1963): 492-95.

27. C. S. Ough and M. A. Amerine, "Effect of Subjects' Sex, Experience, and Training on Their Red Wine Color-Preference Patterns," *Perceptual and Motor Skills* 30, no. 2 (1970): 395-98.

28. F. D. Lawson, "Hair Color, Personality, and the Observer," *Psychological Reports* 28, no. 1 (1971): 311-22.

29. M. N. Bartholet, "Effects of Color," *Nursing Outlook,* October 1968, p. 51.

30. M. E. Chevreul, *The Principles of Harmony and Contrast of Color and Their Applications to the Arts,* based on the first English edition of 1854 as translated from the first French edition of 1839 (New York: Reinhold Publishing Corp., 1967).

31. Albers, *Interaction,* pp. 54-58.

32. For a discussion of the work of E. H. Weber and G. T. Fechner, see R. S. Woodworth and H. Schlosberg, *Experimental Psychology* (New York: Henry Holt & Co., 1956).

Name Index

Aaronson, B., 125, 126, 156
Adler, L., 16-17, 144, 145
Albers, J., 86, 119, 123, 140-41, 156, 158
Allesch, G. J. von, 3, 143
Allport, 70
Alschuler, R., 14, 144
Amerine, M. A., 132, 158
Aristotle, 1
Asch, M. J., 60, 149
Atkinson, J. W., 146, 150

Baker, E., 28, 146
Bannatyne, A., 21, 145
Barnard, J. E., 152
Barnes, R. B., 95, 154
Bartholet, M. N., 133, 158
Berg, H. W., 131, 158
Bezold, 3

Bjerstadt, A., 68, 150
Blank, H. R., 80, 153
Bliss, L. S., 75, 76, 151
Boynton, P., 28, 146
Brown, B. B., 82-83, 153
Brucke, 3
Buckout, R., 96, 155
Bullough, E., 4-5, 144

Calef, V., 79, 152
Cantril, H., 59, 149
Catford, J. C., 151
Chandler, A. R., 5, 144
Chapanis, A., 53-54, 90, 149, 154
Chase, J. A., 18, 144
Chevreul, M. E., 3, 140-41, 143, 158
Chiba, Y., 147
Child, I. L., 18, 42, 145, 147
Chongourian, A., 36, 37, 147

NAME INDEX

Claparede, 99
Clark, K., 45, 148
Cleveland, S., 71, 151
Clynes, M., 84
Cohn, J., 3
Compton, N. H., 70-71, 150, 151
Cook, 42
Cook, M., 144
Couch, A., 60, 149
Crane, R. R., 69, 150
Crannell, C. W., 24-25, 145

Dale, P., 76, 151
Dement, W., 152
Descoeudres, 66
Diserens, C. M., 98, 99, 155
Domingos, W. R., 86, 153
Downey, J. E., 99, 155
Duncan, I., 114
Dunker, K., 130, 157
Dunlap, W. J., 128, 157
Dworine, 89

Edwards, A. L., 61, 150
Einstein, 101
Ellis, W. D., 155
Endacott, J. L., 28, 146

Faas, L. A., 91
Faraday, 101
Fechner, G. T., 141, 158
Fisher, C., 152
Fisher, S., 71, 151
Fortier, R. H., 26, 28-30, 145, 146
Foster, D., 130, 157
Franzen, R., 128, 157
Freud, S., 32, 77-79, 114, 152

Gattegno, C., 24, 145
Gerard, R., 85, 153
Gibson, J. E., 154
Gilbert, J. G., 90, 154

Glick, I. D., 45, 148
Gobetz, W., 70
Goethe, J. W. von, 2, 143
Goldfarb, W., 25, 145
Goldstein, K., 56, 84-85, 149, 153
Gramza, H. G., 144
Grant, C. W., 60, 149
Greenacre, P., 79, 152
Grunewald, K., 89, 154
Guilford, J. P., 4, 54, 55, 56-57,
        126-27, 129, 144, 149, 156, 157

Hall, C., 76, 77, 152
Halpern, L., 86, 153
Hansen, B., 131, 156, 158
Hansen, J. A., 18, 145
Hapten, K., 89, 153
Hardy, J. D., 95, 154, 155
Hattwick, L., 14, 144
Heidbreder, E., 75, 151
Heiss, R., 64, 143, 149, 150
Helson, H., 5, 144
Hering, 88
Herschel, E. W., 94
Herschel, W., 94
Hertz, M. R., 28, 101, 146
Hilgard, E. R., 103, 156
Hodgman, C. D., 97, 155
Hoffer, A., 116, 156
Hoffman, A., 116
Holtzman, 63
Honkavaara, S., 66-67, 150
Hornbeck, F. W., 18, 145
Husband, R., 80, 152

Irwin, M. H., 44, 148
Itten, J., 119-21

James, W. T., 86, 153
Johnson, A. H., 131, 157
Josephine, 115
Judd, D. B., 53, 148

Jung, C. G., 79, 117, 156

Kadzin, P., 71-72, 151
Kahn, E., 76, 77, 152
Kanig, J. L., 130, 156
Kastl, A. J., 42, 147
Katz, D., 89, 154
Kellagham, T., 43, 148
Kelly, K. L., 53, 148
Kennedy, J. F., 116
Kenniston, L., 60, 149
Klopfer, B., 25, 145
Knapp, P. H., 76, 79, 152
Knapp, R. H., 34-35, 64-65, 146, 150
Koffa, 101
Kohler, 101
Kolin, M., 84
Krause, B., 25, 145
Kraut, 70
Kronenberg, B., 150
Kugelmass, S., 86, 153
Kuleshova, R., 93

Ladd-Franklin, 88
Lawler, C. O., 56, 149
Lawler, E. E., 56, 149
Lawson, F. D., 132, 158
Lemkau, P., 150
Levy, B. I., 68, 150
Lewin, K., 101, 102, 155
Likert, 42
Lindauer, M., 33-34, 35, 36, 146
Lindzey, 70
Lovett Doust, J. W., 76, 152
Lowenfeld, 18, 144
Luce, C. B., 132
Luscher, M., 58, 149

McClelland, D. C., 35, 66, 146, 150
McCulloch, R., 71-72, 151
McLaughlin, D. H., 44, 148
Makous, W. L., 96-97, 155

Maslow, 70
Maxwell, 101
Mead, M., 36
Middleton, W. C., 54, 152
Miron, M. S., 40, 147
Mohammed, 51
Money, J. 145
Monk, T., 123
Monnier, M., 27, 146
Monroe, W. S., 76, 152
Moon, P., 124-25, 156
Morland, J. K., 47, 148
Mudge, E. L., 98, 155
Munsell, A. H., 4, 122, 144
Murstein, B. I., 72, 151
Muschenheim, C., 95, 154
Myer-Briggs, 79

Nakshian, J. S., 85, 153
Napoleon, 115
Newton, I., 2

Ogletree, E., 148
Oppel, T. W., 95, 155
Orr, D. B., 155
Osgood, C. E., 37-40, 55, 58, 127, 147, 156
Osmond, H., 117, 156
Osmundsen, J. A., 153
Ostwald, W., 4, 36, 37, 122, 144, 156
Ough, C. S., 132, 158
Oyama, T., 41, 147

Pangborn, R. M., 131, 157, 158
Paterson, D. G., 128, 157
Pavlov, 126
Petrie, A., 71-72, 151
Pevzener, A. I., 74, 151
Pfistek, M., 23, 58, 149
Phillips, E., 29, 146
Piaget, J., 12-13, 149
Pollock, J., 124

NAME INDEX

Price, A. C., 89, 154

Renninger, C. A., 47, 48, 148
Richards, W., 87, 154
Rickers-Ovsiankina, M., x, xi, 143
Rorschach, H., x, 10, 25-31, 58, 62-
    63, 70, 72, 73, 105, 143, 145,
    146, 150
Rousseau, 32
Rubin, M. L., 87, 154
Rudsill, H., 19, 145

Salvia, J., 19, 145
Schachtel, E., x, xi, 143
Schaie, K. W., xi, 10, 58, 64, 126,
    143, 144, 149, 150, 156
Schall, L. R., 147
Schiffman, G., 145
Schlosberg, H., 158
Schutz, H. G., 157
Scott, Ian, 149
Selby, S. M., 155
Serpell, R., 43, 147
Sharpe, D. T., 17-18, 48, 58, 60, 69,
    100, 109-11, 149
Sherif, M., 59, 149
Shugerts, J., 19, 145
Singer, K., 99, 155
Small, V. H., 155
Smets, Gerda, 81, 153
Smirnov, M., 94
Smith, P. C., 54, 57, 129, 148, 157
Spencer, D., 124-25, 156
Starch, D., 128, 157
Stromberg, E., 29, 146
Suci, G. J., 147, 156
Suinn, R. M., 79, 152

Tanaka, Y., 40, 147
Tannenbaum, P. H., 147, 156
Taylor, C., 123
Thomas, D., 25, 145
Tinker, M. A., 128, 157
Tolor, A., 74-75, 151
Tucker, W. T., 40, 147
Twitchell-Allen, 68

Van Cott, H. P., 155
Venus de Milo, 50
Vernon, 70
Vinci, L. da, 1

Waaler, G. H. M., 87, 154
Wadsworth, B., 28, 146
Warner, L., 128, 157
Weast, R. C., 155
Weber, E. H. 141, 155
Wertheimer, M., 101, 155
Wheeler, J. C., 91, 154
White, H. L., 89, 154
Wig, E. H., 75, 76, 151
Williams, J. E., 42, 45-47, 48, 147, 148
Wilson, G. D., 82, 153
Winick, C., 49, 148
Witt, P. A., 144
Woodmansee, 42
Woodworth, R. S., 158
Wundt, 3

Yazmajian, R., 79, 152
Young-Helmholtz, 88
Youtz, R. P., 94, 95, 96, 154
Yu, K. C., 151

Zavala, A., 97, 155

Subject Index

Achievement motivation, 34-35
Achromatic color, 5, 125
Achromatic representations, 63, 72-73
Activity (A) factors, 38-39, 46-47
Adaptation, 5
Advertising, 128
Aesthetic measure, 124-25
Aesthetic preferences, 12-14, 65. *See also* Color preference; Color-form preference; Form preference
Affective factors, 3, 4, 11, 14, 15, 27, 29, 38, 41, 42, 47, 59, 69, 72, 126, 129
Africa, 33, 44, 116
Afterimage, 5, 88, 118-19
Age factors, 7-32, 37, 43, 44, 45, 47-48, 68, 75, 78, 80, 90, 136,
137. *See also* Children in testing; Maturation
Allport, Vernon, Lindzey Study of Values, 70
America. *See* United States
Americans, 37, 40-41, 42-43
Anomaloscope, 87, 89
Aphasiacs, 75
Arabs, 50, 51
Arousal value, 82, 83, 85
Artists, 1, 2, 115, 116-18, 124
Asia, 33, 50
Association(s), 4-5, 7, 15, 19, 21, 22, 23, 24-25, 46-47, 49-51, 55, 56, 58, 79, 82, 84, 86, 91-93, 105, 110, 122, 123, 125-26, 128, 129-35, 137. *See also* Connotative meanings; Symbolism
Attitudes, 36, 42, 45

SUBJECT INDEX

Augmenters, 71-72
Australia, 50
Autism, 73-74

Background color, 25, 138, 139
Battery of tests, 70, 75
Beige, 17, 69, 107, 114, 115, 138
Biological color, 1, 89
Biological factors, 7, 11, 19, 51, 54,
      55, 56, 66, 69, 87, 89-90, 98,
      127-28. See also Physiology
Bipolar adjectives, 38-39, 58, 132-33
Black, 12, 17, 18, 25, 41, 42, 45-48,
      49-51, 55, 57, 64, 73, 74, 93,
      96, 99, 103, 125, 126, 134,
      135, 136, 137, 139
Black and white, 25, 77, 93, 103,
      128, 137
"Blacks," 48. See also Negroes
Blind(ness), 80, 91, 98, 100. See
      also Colorblind(ness)
Blue, 2, 9, 15-16, 17, 22, 33, 34, 35,
      36, 37, 41, 49, 51, 54, 55, 56,
      57, 61, 62, 63, 64, 65, 68, 69,
      74, 75, 81, 82, 83, 84, 87, 90,
      91, 92, 93, 94, 96, 97, 107,
      114, 120, 125, 126, 128, 129,
      131, 133, 136
Blue-green, 35, 36, 37, 41, 74, 78,
      87, 120, 121, 125
Blue-purple, 41, 70
Blue-violet, 120, 121
Blue-yellow blindness, 88
Body-image, 71
Brain damage, 23, 75, 84-85, 86
Bright colors, 34, 63, 71, 86, 117,
      135, 136, 137
Brightness, 2, 4, 17, 18-19, 24, 41,
      42, 54, 56-57, 82, 99, 105, 107,
      115, 119, 129, 137
Brightness contrast, 128-29
Brown, 17, 42, 45-46, 51, 55, 56, 64,
      92, 96, 99, 114, 132, 135, 136

Buddhists, 50
Burma, 50

Caucasians, 42, 45-48, 91
Central America, 51
Ceylon, 50
Cherry red, 128-29
Children in testing, 7-32, 33, 56, 66,
      72, 73, 98
Chinese, 46-47, 49, 91
Chroma, 19, 129
Chromatic representations, 63, 72-73
Climate. See Weather
Closure, 102, 106-7
Clothes, 49, 51, 69, 70-71, 80, 136
Color
   coding (racial), 42, 47, 48
   consultants, 54-55
   dimensionality. See Dimensions of
      color
   disability, 25, 74
   discrimination. See Colorblind
      (ness); Perception
   dominance, 8-12, 23, 31-32, 44, 75
   harmony. See Harmony
   hearing, 98, 99
   matching, 8, 19, 90, 108
   meanings. See Association(s);
      Connotative meanings; Symbolism
   memory, 86
   mood, 5
   names, 42, 45, 46, 53-54
   naming, 19, 31, 47, 76
   orientation. See Color dominance
   pairs, 3, 88-89
   preference(s), 3, 4, 8, 9, 12, 13, 14,
      17, 18, 19, 20, 23, 33, 34, 35,
      37, 38, 42-45, 49, 54, 56-57,
      58, 66, 72, 127, 130, 131, 132,
      135, 136, 137. See also Color
      dominance; Color-form preference
   response (C), 10, 25-26, 27, 28,
      30-31, 33, 42, 59, 63-64, 70,

99, 123, 126-28
retention, 76
revolution, 4, 115-16, 118, 123
shock, 62, 70, 72
smell, 5, 98, 100
sound, 5, 98, 99
space, 4, 54, 123
stress factor (C-factor), 73
systems, 122
taste, 98-99
temperature, 5, 94-95. *See also*
  Cool colors; Warm colors
thresholds, 74
trends, 113-28
usage, 1, 91-93, 114, 115, 118, 122,
  123, 124, 126, 130-31, 133,
  134-35
vision, 22, 74, 86-88. *See also*
  Colorblind(ness); Perception
weight, 5, 41, 123. *See also*
  Potency (P) factor
wheel, 3, 118, 123, 127
Color-affect theory, 63
Colorblind(ness), 19, 21-22, 84,
  88-89, 90-91
Color combinations, visibility of, 107
Color-dominant personality, 11-12
"Colored" persons. *See* Negroes
Color-flavor associations, 129-32
Color-form
  classification, 64-65
  dominance, 10, 11, 75
  index, 32
  influence, 10
  levels of abstraction, 8
  perception, 23
  persons, 12
  position, 18
  preference, 7, 8-12, 22-23, 34,
    43, 54, 55
  response (CF), 10, 26, 27, 28,
    30-31
  theory, 32

Color in dreams, 76-80
Color-matching tasks, 73-74
Color-mood associations, 56
Color-word association, 19, 22, 125-26
Color-reactors, 66-67
Color-taste associations, 129-32
Communality of color preference, 54,
  55, 126, 127
Complementary colors, 3, 118-19,
  120-23
Complementary color-harmony school,
  122-23
Conditioning, 7, 23
Connotative meanings, 19, 38-39,
  45, 47, 48, 58. *See also* Associ-
  ation(s); Meaning; Symbolism
Continuity, 102, 106
Contrast, 3, 13, 14, 18, 88, 119, 128-
  29
Cool colors, 2, 5, 15, 17, 18, 41, 62,
  63, 68, 70, 81, 105, 106-7
Cream (color), 57
Creativity, 11, 14, 31-32, 67, 69, 123
Cue-names, 139-40
Cues, 23-25, 110
Cultural differences, 16, 33-51, 54,
  55, 56, 74, 126, 127

Danes, 45-46
Dark color(s), 18, 51, 103, 125, 135
Deaf(ness), 12, 43
Department stores, 109-10, 137, 138
Depression, 55, 61, 63, 64, 125,
  135-36
Depression (1929-39), 114-15
Delinquents. *See* Juvenile delinquents
Design, 23, 57, 71, 101, 102, 104-6,
  108-11, 117, 119, 123, 136,
  138-41. *See also* Figure-ground;
  Form; Interior Design; Pattern
Development of color and form pref-
  erences, 7, 8, 10-11, 12, 13,
  17, 18-19, 20, 22, 25

SUBJECT INDEX

Dichromatism, 22, 88
Dimensions of color, 10, 41, 54, 91. *See also* Brightness; Hue; Saturation
Distance (D) factor, 38-39
Dominance. *See* Color dominance; Color-form dominance; Form dominance; Mixed dominance; Number dominance
Dreams, 76-80
Dyes, 2-3, 115

East Indians, 45-46
Educational factors, 43, 44, 75. *See also* Learning
Educational implications, 7, 12, 20, 22, 24-25, 31-32
Electroencephalogram (EEG), 82-84
Emotional factors, 28, 68, 69, 70, 71, 73, 79-80, 128. *See also* Affective factors; Association(s); Expression of emotions
England, 43, 66-67
Enuretic children, 30
Epileptics, 30, 93
Europe, 33, 44, 50, 58
Evaluation (E) factor, 38-39, 40-41
Experience, 7, 12, 22, 54, 102
Expression of emotions, 14-16, 22, 56, 59, 63, 67, 82-86, 133-34

Factor loadings, 39, 40, 41, 63
Fashion therapy, 71. *See also* Clothes
"Field," 101, 102, 110-11
Figure-ground, 25, 66, 70, 90, 101-9
"Finger vision," 93-98
Flag colors, 33-36, 51
Food coloring, 129-32
Form
    dimensionality, 10
    discrimination, 75, 98
    dominance, 8-12, 31, 32
    preference, 8, 43, 44-45

response, 123
sorting, 44-45
Form-color response (FC), 10, 26, 27, 28, 30-31
Form-dominant personality, 11-12, 32
Form-matching, 76
Form-reactors, 66-68
Forstman Museum, 114
Furniture arrangement, 108-9

Gay Nineties, 125
Genetics. *See* Biological factors
Geographic influences, 33-34, 137
Germans, 45-46, 64, 91
Gestalt psychology, 66, 101-11
Gold, 50, 99
Goldenrod (color), 128
Gray, 9, 17, 41, 46, 47, 49, 51, 55, 69, 88, 92, 96, 114, 115, 122, 125, 126, 134, 135, 138, 139
Gray-black, 118, 121
Grayish green, 114
Grayish yellow, 88
Green, 2, 16, 17, 18, 22, 25, 33, 34, 35, 36, 37, 41, 47, 49, 50, 54, 55, 61, 62, 64, 68, 69, 70, 74, 75, 82, 84, 85, 86, 87, 90, 92, 96, 107, 114, 118, 120, 121, 122, 124, 125, 126, 129, 131, 133, 134, 136
Green-blue, 37
Green-yellow, 54, 70

Harmony, 2, 3, 4, 12, 13, 14, 115, 119, 120, 123, 124-25
High colors, 64
Hindus, 50
History, 1-5, 19, 27, 35, 89, 94, 101, 113-16
Homeostasis, 135-36
Hue(s), 2, 5, 9, 22, 41, 42, 54, 56, 81, 82, 91, 104, 105, 107
Hue preference, 9, 17, 18, 19

Hysteric, 30

India, 43, 50, 51
Indians (North American), 47, 91
Indigo, 118
Indonesia, 50
Intellectual factors, 7, 8, 11, 13, 23, 26, 31, 43, 123
Intelligence, 69, 70
Interior design, 102, 104-6, 108-11
Iraq, 50
Iran, 36, 50
Israel, 49

Japan, 40-41, 50
Jordan, 50
Juvenile delinquents, 23, 27-30, 32, 71-72

Khaki, 114
Kuwait, 36

Language, 40, 46
Laos, 50
Latin America, 33, 50
Lavender, 114
Laws of color, 2, 118, 141
Learning, 7, 23-25, 27, 32, 54, 92-93, 94, 106, 124, 126, 127, 131
    See also Educational factors;
    Educational implications
Lebanese, 36, 37
Liberia, 44
Light colors, 18, 42, 51, 103, 125
Lights and filters, 74, 81, 83, 85-86, 117
Lilac, 17, 87
Low colors, 64
Luminosity, 3, 13, 19
Lysergic acid diethylamide (LSD), 99, 116, 117

Magenta, 24, 114

Mailings, 128-29
Market research, ix, 57, 110
Maturation, 7, 8, 9, 11, 14, 18-19, 26, 31, 67, 90. See also Age factors; Development of color and form preferences
Meanings, 4, 34, 48, 54. See also Association(s); Connotative meanings; Symbolism
Mentally retarded children. See Retardates
Mexicans, 91
Middle East, 16, 33
Mixed dominance, 8
Moderates, 71-72
Monochromatism, 22, 88, 89, 108

N achievement, 34-35, 65-66
Nay-sayers, 60-61
Negroes, 42, 45-46, 48, 91
Nigerians, 43
North America, 49, 51, 54, 113
Number dominance, 9
Number preference, 44

Olive green, 114
Orange, 2, 12, 17, 21, 36, 41, 47, 49, 54, 55, 63, 64, 69, 70, 81, 87, 96, 107, 114, 118, 120, 121, 122, 124, 125, 126, 130, 131, 132, 133
Orange-red, 99
Orange-yellow, 70
Organics, 30-31, 75, 89
Ostwald color notations, 36, 37

Pakistan, 50
Pastels, 105, 108, 115, 136, 137
Pattern, 14, 103, 104, 105. See also Design; Form
Perception, 7, 10, 43, 53, 71, 74, 81-100, 101-3, 105, 140-41
Perceptual immediacy, 44

SUBJECT INDEX

Perceptual types, 70-71

Personality, 7, 11, 12, 14, 23, 26, 27-28, 30, 31-32, 43, 53-80, 92-93, 132-34

Phonics System, 24

Physics, 1, 2, 86, 87, 94-97, 101, 102, 109

Physiology, 4, 5, 56, 63-64, 69, 77, 82, 83, 86, 106, 118-19, 135-36. See also Biological factors

Pink, 12, 53, 93, 99, 132, 133, 134

Pleasant-unpleasant dimensions, 57

Politics, 50-51, 67

Potency (P) factor, 38-39, 40-41, 47

Practical applications of color, 55, 128-40

Preferences. See Aesthetic preferences Color preference; Color-form preference; Form preference; Hue preference; Number preference; Saturation preferences; Size preference; Skin color preference

Primary colors, 41, 136

Psychedelic movement, 99, 116-18

Psychotic-tending persons, 60-61

Puerto Ricans, 37

Pure color responses. See Color response

Purple, 2, 37, 41, 47, 50, 55, 64, 70, 92, 93, 96, 107, 114, 125, 126, 132, 134

Quantification, 4, 5, 124-25. See also Physics

Quiescent Fifties, 125

Race, 36, 42-49

Racetracks, 138-39

Realism in representation, 13, 19-21

Red, 2, 9, 12, 14-15, 17, 18, 22, 23, 25, 33-34, 35, 36, 37, 41, 42, 45-47, 51, 53, 54, 55, 56, 61, 62, 63, 64, 65, 68, 69, 70, 74, 75, 79, 80, 81, 82, 84, 85, 86, 90, 91, 93, 94, 96, 97, 106, 107, 109, 114, 118, 120, 122, 125, 126, 127, 128-29, 131, 132, 133, 134, 136

Red-green blindness, 88

Red-orange, 120, 121

Red-purple, 41, 126

Reducers, 71-72

Red-violet, 120, 121

Red-yellow, 35

Red-yellow-orange, 15, 17

Religious factors, 34-35, 36, 48, 49, 50, 51

Response bias, 59-61

Retardates, 19, 21-23

Roaring Twenties, 114

Russia. See Soviet Union

Saturated color(s), 5, 57, 61, 63, 70, 71, 73

Saturation, 2, 4, 17, 18-19, 22, 41, 42-43, 54, 56-57, 91, 107-8, 129

Saturation preferences, 18-19

Schizophrenics, 61, 64, 72-74

Semantic Differential (SD), 37-42, 47, 55, 58, 63, 68, 133

Semantic space, 38-39

Sex differences, 10, 17, 18, 19, 21-22, 36, 37, 43, 44, 54, 56, 62, 78, 80, 88, 90, 91, 126, 132, 137

Similarity, 102, 105-6

Size preference, 9, 43-44

Skin color preference, 42, 45-46

Socioeconomic factors, 28, 35, 61, 67, 136, 137

Sorting by color, number, and forms, 44-45

South America, 16, 51

Soviet Union, 92, 114

Spain, 49

Spectrum, 2, 14-15, 17, 36, 53, 55, 87, 94, 96-97, 128
Style, artistic, 12, 13, 14
Sudan, 50
Supergraphics, 136, 138
Switzerland, 58
Symbolism, 1, 2, 9, 40, 45, 46-51, 55, 58, 77-78, 79, 117, 127, 128. *See also* Connotative meanings; Meanings
Synesthesia, 5, 93, 98-100, 116

Taiwan, 74
Tan, 115
Tests, 7, 8-31, 33, 37, 43, 66-67, 70, 75, 135, 138
    California Psychological Inventory, 70
    Color Drawing Test, 75
    Color Pyramid Test (CPT), 10, 23, 58, 64-65
    Compton Fabric Preference Test, 70, 71
    Dermo-optical perception (DOP) test, 94-95
    Descoeudres' Color-Form Test, 66-67
    Edwards Personal Preference Schedule, 61
    Fruit Tree Experiment, 16-17, 21
    Galvanic Skin Response (GSR), 68, 82
    Holtzman inkblots, 63
    Intelligence, 11
    Kraut Personal Preference, 70
    Lie detector, 68, 82
    Lowenfeld Mosaic Test, 18
    The Luscher Color Test, 58
    Maslow Security-Insecurity Inventory, 70
    Memory-for-Designs, 89
    Minnesota Multi-phasic Personality Inventory, 60, 65, 70

Organic Integrity Test, 75
Paired Color Pattern Device, 68
Reaction-time, 86
Rorschach Inkblot Method, 10, 25-26, 27-31, 58, 62, 63, 70, 72. *See also* references under Color response; Color-form response; Form-color response
Self-testing, 58-59
Spiral Aftereffects, 89
Strong Vocational Interest Inventory, 65
Tartan Test, 65
Thematic Apperception Test, 72
Three Dimensional Personality Test, 68
Word-color association, 19
Theories
    of aesthetic measure, 124
    of behavior, 5
    of biological determinants, 56
    of color, 1, 2, 5, 140
    of color-affect, 63
    of colorblindness, 88-89
    of color-form, 32
    of color vision, 88-89
    of preference patterns, 11
Time expression, 81
Trichomat, 88
Turks, 91
Turquoise. *See* Green-blue

"Unique green," 87
United States, 33, 36, 64, 115
Unsaturated color(s), 54, 56

Vectors and valences, 109-11
Victorian period, 113-14
Vietnamese, 42-43
Violet, 17, 49, 54, 69, 114, 118, 120, 121, 122

Warm colors, 2, 15, 17, 18, 41, 62,

169

SUBJECT INDEX

Warm colors (*continued*)
  63, 68, 70, 71, 81, 105, 106-7
Wavelength(s), 47, 54, 81, 94-95,
  96
Weather, 49, 51, 53, 94
Weber-Fechner Law, 141
Weight, 5, 26, 41. *See also* Potency
  (P) factor
White, 18, 24, 25, 34, 41, 42, 45-
  48, 49-50, 64, 74, 86, 92, 93,
  96, 97, 103, 106, 107, 109,
  114, 115, 122, 125, 126, 127,
  128, 129, 131, 132, 133, 134,
  138
Wine (color), 114
Wordless Book, 48
Words in color, 24
Working titles, 139-40

World War I, 114
World War II, 50, 115

Yea-sayers, 60-61
Yellow, 2, 9, 17, 18, 33, 34, 35, 37,
  41, 42, 45-47, 49, 50, 53, 54,
  55, 56, 61, 62, 63, 64, 68, 69,
  70, 75, 81, 86, 87, 88, 90, 91,
  92, 96, 97, 107, 118, 120, 121,
  122, 125, 126, 128, 129, 130,
  132, 133
Yellow-green, 36, 41, 70, 120, 121,
  125, 126
Yellow-orange, 41, 70, 120, 121
Yellow-red, 126
Yellow-violet, 120

Zambian, 43